WHAT YOUR BODY NEEDS IN FLIGHT

You need to drink a cupful of mineral water about once an hour. Your water intake should be inversely proportional to the load factor of the aircraft—that is, you need less if the flight is full and more if it is half-empty or empty. A banana, which contains complex sugars that are digested at different rates, provides a sustained stream of energy—a bonus for passengers with tough schedules awaiting them at their destination.

Books by Farrol Kahn

Airwise
The Curse of Icarus
Why Flying Endangers Your Health
Arrive in Better Shape

DISCLAIMER:

Every effort has been made to ensure that the information presented in this book is accurate. Advice from a book has limitations, however, and cannot take into account the specific circumstances of each individual passenger. Any advice offered here is not intended to replace counsel given by competent medical personnel. If you have a health problem that leaves you with any doubts about flying, please consult your physician or health practitioner.

ARRIVE IN BETTER SHAPE

How to Avoid Jet Lag and Travel Stress

Farrol Kahn

HarperPaperbacks
A Division of HarperCollinsPublishers

HarperPaperbacks *A Division of* HarperCollins*Publishers*
10 East 53rd Street, New York, N.Y. 10022

An edition of this book was published in 1995 by Thorsons, an imprint of HarperCollins*Publishers* in Great Britain.

Cover photographs courtesy of Delta Airlines

First HarperPaperbacks printing: July 1996

Printed in the United States of America

HarperPaperbacks and colophon are trademarks of HarperCollins*Publishers*

❖ 10 9 8 7 6 5 4 3 2 1

To Samuel and Tessa

CONTENTS

Acknowledgments

My thanks are due to many people who helped in the preparation of this book. In particular I am indebted to Dr. Tony Andrews, Dr. Jeffrey Aronson, Professor J. Grimley Evans, Dr. Jocelyn Morris, Dr. Eric Newsholme, Professor Jasper Griffin, Dr. David Moore, Dr. Paul Salkovskis and Dr. Robert Turner of the University of Oxford; Dr. Chris Bates, Professor Kay-Tee Khaw and Professor James Fitzsimons of the University of Cambridge; Richard Collins and Dr. William Needleman of *Pall Europe*; Sir Norman and Lady Foster; Doug Jagger of *British Aerospace Airbus*; Dr. Edwin Kenyon and Professor Isaac Marks of the Institute of Psychiatry; James Nicholls of Avalon Studios; Toni Noble, Dr. Ken Shaw of the National Radiological Protection Board; Dr. James Snedden and Dr. Ian Stratford of the Medical Research Council Radiobiology Laboratory; Dr. Duncan P. Thomas and Professor Jim Watson of Guy's Hospital.

I also wish to acknowledge the assistance of Dr. Stephanie Amiel, Professor Josephine Arendt of Surrey University, Dr. Helen Ashworth, Dr. Anthony Fry, Dr. Duncan Geddes; Dr. Richard Harding, Peta Pascoe and Dr. Alexander MacMillan of the RAF Institute of Aviation Medicine; Dr. David Jones; Professor Ian Macdonald and Dr. Joan Bassey of the University of Nottingham; Dr. Kevin Maynard of AEA Technology;

Dr. Mark Rosekind of NASA-Ames; Dr. Ann Sharpley, Dr. Andrew Shelling, Penny Simpson, Dr. John Stradling, Captain Tim Ward and Professor Brian Whipp of St. George's Hospital.

It is a pleasure to acknowledge the generous help of Yolanda Foster, Dean Breest, *British Airways*, *Delta Air Lines*, the Pierre Hotel (New York), Holiday Inn Crowne Plaza (Los Angeles), Sebel Town House and Nikko Hotel (Sydney), Regent Hotel (Auckland) and the Ritz Carlton (Atlanta). In addition, thanks to Todd Clay, Margaret Cooper, David Fleming, Sarah Johnson, Michael Jones, Dick Koscher, Captain Jock Lowe, Captain Geoffrey Mussett, Paulette O'Donnell, Dave Rowland and Ian Webster.

Introduction

*Safe and efficient international jet service
began in earnest around 1957. That's
an interesting moment in the history
of human passivity.*
PAUL FUSSELL, *ABROAD*

The experience of flying has been made as bland and
routine as possible. In fact, the impression created is
that we are not up in the air at all. Everything about the
interior of an aircraft is made to resemble other forms
of surface transport—a bus or a train, for example.

We usually enter through a tube from a gate or waiting room and are hardly aware of the unusual features
of the plane. Indeed, we are ushered on board like a
herd of blinkered horses. Our perceptions are narrowed
and limited and, once inside the cabin, we spend a passive interlude between airports. Food, muzak, movies,
martinis and even shopping facilities are provided to
distract us from the reality that we are actually flying
high above the earth, among the clouds.

"Passive flyers" is an apt description of many passengers today. Unlike pilots and copilots, who are at the
sharp end, we are kept in a state of sensory deprivation.
As a consequence, if we show any emotions they are
usually negative: boredom (induced by familiarity), irritation or anger (at a canceled or delayed flight), and

insecurity or fear (brought on by sensitivity or the mistaken idea that flying is dangerous). Rarely do we feel the excitement, stimulation or awe that flying should inspire.

This book is an attempt to redress the balance. Obviously I cannot strap you into the copilot's seat or take you into a steep, tight curve to experience the unique sensations of *G*—the centrifugal force that greys your vision, fuzzes your brain and heats up your feet. But I *can* introduce you to a world you may not realize exists.

Take the aircraft you travel in: As an indoor space it is part modern, sealed building (with its own heating, ventilation and air-conditioning systems) and part manned spacecraft just like the ones that have taken astronauts to the moon. If you are surprised by this you may also be surprised to learn that the flight environment is unique and makes unusual demands on your body.

We all know that our ankles and feet swell during a flight. But did you know that the air in your stomach does the same? Or that your heartbeat and breathing rate increase and, in spite of the cool air in the cabin, you sweat as profusely as if you were in the tropics? And why are we exhausted by flying when we spend most of the time sitting down?

Some people also suffer the embarrassing experience of suddenly being overcome by giddiness and keeling over. Can we prevent this common problem on long-haul flights? The answer is Yes, and the remedy is so simple that anyone can take advantage of it.

What about "flying healthy"—is there such a thing? This book explains how different aircraft models and certain parts of a plane are healthier to travel in than others, and provides scads of advice on aviation health for children, the elderly, asthmatics, people with diabetes, and for business and leisure passengers.

Aerophobia, or fear of flying, is familiar to most of us. However, few realize that this emotion is intertwined with its opposite: the joy of flying. In fact, these contradictory emotions have roots in our psyche as deep as those of love and hate. This goes some way toward explaining the fact that even active flyers can suffer from aerophobia. Pilots as well, from the senior to the most junior, can exhibit symptoms of hyperventilation, nightmares or vertigo.

Then there is the word that is synonymous with air travel: Jetlag. It has assumed a wide band of meanings—from swollen ankles, earache, temporary deafness, dryness of the skin, airport stress and the effects of crossing the international dateline, to alcoholic excess, forgetfulness, fatigue, depression and any condition suffered after a flight. Strictly speaking, jetlag has quite a narrow definition: It is the disruption of our 24-hour clock, our biological rhythms. By clarifying this we are able to deal effectively with it and with all the other symptoms affecting our health during and after a flight.

How to Use this Book

This book is divided into three sections. "The Best Way to Fly" offers instant benefits whether you read it weeks before departure or en route. The strategies outlined in this section's pre-flight, in-flight and post-flight stages are simple to use. Choose several from each stage—using them in combination will produce the best results and can make all the difference between arriving irritated and exhausted or positive, relaxed and stimulated.

The second section is an A-to-Z of air-travel subjects, including advice where appropriate. Here you will find everything you need to know about flying healthy: The Wonder Juice (the result of five years' research through medical archives); entries covering the physiological changes that your body undergoes in-flight (including Blood Circulation, Gas Expansion, Humidity, Oxygen Deficiency and Stress); and little-known facts about in-flight Meals, Airline Seats, Medications and Alcohol. Practical issues are addressed in articles on Pregnancy, Exercise, Supplemental Oxygen, Mountain Sickness, the effects of air travel on diving holidays (Decompression Sickness) and methods of inducing Sleep, the best Flying Clothes to wear, and how to handle Stopovers. For the amorous, there is an arcane aphrodisiac described in the entry on Sex. There are also items on certain engineering features that can affect your health, such as Cabin Air Quality and Pressure Cabin, as well as a discussion of the effect of flying on the psyche in entries such as Aviation Psychology and Safe Space.

The third section focuses on aviation from its mythical origins to the present day. Within a short space of time there has been phenomenal success both in the air and in space. Some 200 astronauts and cosmonauts have popped in and out of space, where they have spent a total of 7,700 Earth-days. *Concorde*, too, has flown more times at twice the speed of sound than all the military high-performance jets combined, and is credited with over 100,000 hours at Mach 2. However, it appears that many people have scarcely had the chance to assimilate this progress, let alone to appreciate fully that the dream of flight has been fulfilled. This has manifested itself in a strange way, which "Enjoy Your Flight!" explores.

Throughout the book there are nine scattered "case studies" from a spectrum of professional flyers including:

a vice chairman of Merrill Lynch
a partner in Goldman Sachs
the chairman of ICI
a six-million mile flyer
the world's No. 1 woman flyer
a top U.S. legal eagle
the owner of the earliest surviving Hotchkiss 1904
and a Californian who is jetlag-free.

Each provides insights into effective air travel, as well as hints on health.

Celebrities, too, reveal some of their flying secrets. Read about Doris Day, Dan Quayle, Douglas Adams, Robert Redford, Caroline Rose Hunt, Tracey Ullman, Pierce Brosnan and the world's oldest air traveler, the 100-year-old Professor Dirk Struik of MIT.

Once the aircraft doors close, the time you spend on board should be relaxing, enjoyable and hopefully inspiring. Air travel is a special activity, not merely a "pause in the day's occupations." You may not be able to control the aircraft, but the aim of this book is to give you control over your body and your mind when you fly—so that you arrive in better shape.

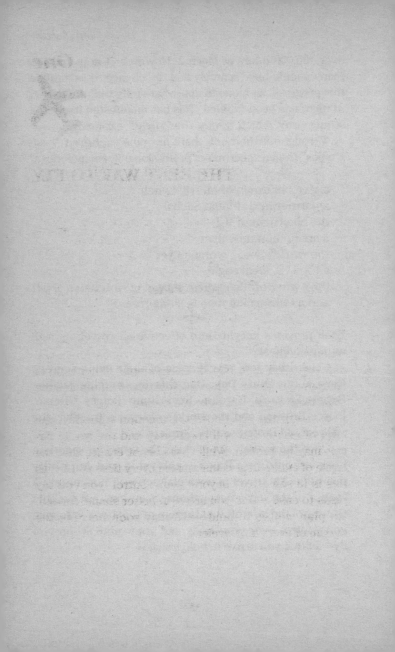

One

THE BEST WAY TO FLY

Flight Plan

When we travel by air (motivational researchers tell us), we enter a "circle of excitement." The circle is composed of several links, each of which stimulates the other two to create "an excited circuit."

If any of the links does not function smoothly, the level of excitement will be affected and the whole circuit may be broken. While you cannot ensure that the circle of excitement is maintained every time you fly, as this is in some part beyond your control, you *can* lay plans to ensure that you arrive in better shape. Indeed, "to plan well is to land well" may soon become the maxim of every air traveler.

PRE-FLIGHT

> *Self-indulgence is what the ancients blithely*
> *called indulging in one's genius.*
> NORMAN DOUGLAS,
> RACONTEUR AND TRAVEL WRITER

There are all sorts of ingenious things you can take with you when you fly, and unusual preparations you can make before you go. I was once involved in conducting a survey of the things passengers consider "essential" when they pack for a long-distance journey. The results were not unexpected: magazines, bestsellers, duty-free alcohol or gifts, toiletry or washbags and patent medicines topped the list.

Among the less commonplace, however, were two which have stuck in my mind: a small torch (flashlight) and sandwiches. One businessperson said he always packed a small torch because he had read somewhere that this could be useful in the event of a hotel fire. And the sandwiches? These were for a woman who swore she never traveled on business or pleasure without them because she disliked airline food and could thus eat whenever she was hungry.

Your travel kit may include its own eccentric or unique items, and you may have a sound reason for including each one. As I do not want to start our journey with excess luggage, however, in this section I want to provide you with a truly essential list of what you need for a healthy, relaxing and enjoyable flight.

These items should make up part of your hand luggage. I myself have got into the habit of traveling with only a hold-all into which I cram everything, including a suit. This saves me having to check anything in or having to wait for it to come down the luggage carousel when I reach my destination. A small suitcase on wheels, such as those favoured by flight attendants, also serves as a good piece of hand luggage.

Essential Items for the Long Haul

CLOTHING The two factors to consider are determined by the cabin environment: your body inflates during a flight, and the cabin air temperature is kept very cool. Therefore, loose casual clothes are a must, as is an extra sweater or pullover for warmth. The well-dressed flight attendants you see on board wear either a larger sized uniform than they really need or one with an elasticated waistband.

Businesspeople should change from their suits to something more casual either in the airport lounge or on board. They should also pack in their hand luggage an extra shirt and underwear as well as any important documents, just in case the luggage they check on board goes astray.

FOOD AND DRINK I should mention at once that I am not advocating that passengers bring their own food on board, but there is an argument for taking specific items which are good for your health and can enhance your recovery from jetlag, fatigue or tension on arrival.

At the top of the list is carrot juice (*see* **The Wonder Juice**), a bottle of flat (not carbonated) mineral water and a banana.

You need to drink a cupful of mineral water about once an hour. Your water intake should be inversely proportional to the load factor of the aircraft—that is, you need less if the flight is full and more if it is half empty or empty. A banana, which contains complex sugars that are digested at different rates, provides a sustained stream of energy—a bonus for passengers with tough schedules awaiting them at their destination. In this respect, passengers have something in common with tennis players: sufficient water can mean the difference between winning or losing matches, and one banana can supply enough energy for a five-set match!

BOOKS AND MAGAZINES Reading material, you may be surprised to learn, can serve other purposes besides entertainment. It can relax you, send you to sleep, be a better way to beat anxiety or aerophobia than several whiskies or mild tranquillizers, or even help you to become a more "active flyer."

One passenger may take along a book on a subject she has always found tedious—say "Studies in Tudor Social History." She begins to yawn after several pages and is asleep in a short time. Fearful flyers, on the other hand, should choose a book or magazine that has the opposite effect. You want to be so engrossed in the contents that you barely notice that the plane has taken off or has been in the air for several hours. There is also the option of taking classic aviation literature (*see* **"Enjoy Your Flight!"**, pages 139–44).

IN-FLIGHT HEALTH KIT This is an unusual item and should not be confused with Amenity Kits, which are "goody bags" given by airlines to passengers in First and Business Class (some airlines, such as *British Airways*, *Finnair* and *Aer Lingus*, also give their Premium passengers interesting health products).

The kit that I have in mind has evolved from the need to counteract the effects of the pressurized cabin as well as to help you once you have arrived at your destination. The contents can vary but may include some or all of the following:

- eye mask
- earplugs
- rehydration gel
- nasal and sinus refresher
- ankle rub made with essential oils that encourage circulation
- aspirins
- vitamins C and E
- essential oils
- anti-diarrhea medicine
- tablets for indigestion (such as *Alka-Seltzer*)
- an acetazolamide if you are going to a mountain resort
- a decongestant spray for those with bad colds (some airlines, such as *British Airways*, always keep this in their in-flight **Medical Kits**).

Dr. Paul Nicholson of SmithKline Beecham finds that large earphones are more effective than earplugs in neutralizing sound on board. He also travels with a lightweight pair of slippers as he feels comfortable in them.

MISCELLANEOUS It is natural to take things which may seem odd or even superfluous to others when you are flying to a foreign country. One woman confessed to me that she feels ready for any contingency if she has her aspirin and mints with her during a flight. There is no reason why you cannot be accompanied by your teddy bear or some other talisman, bring your own Persian silk rug to use in your hotel room or have with you your own bedside alarm clock (a popular choice among businesspeople), if any of these helps you to feel more at ease in your new surroundings. Professor Lynette Unger of Miami University always travels with her lucky rubber vulture as it has kept her safe over the past 25 years of air travel. On the rare occasion when she had forgotten to take her talisman along, at the first sign of turbulence she thought she was going to die. But above all, she was indignant at the fact that she was going to meet her maker sitting next to a vacuum cleaner salesman.

I once met a Sri Lankan duty-free operator who invariably packed his collection of ties with him on his frequent trips. He suffered less from jetlag, he claimed, when he took them along. Indeed, in the hotel business a form of nostalgia has been exploited successfully by companies like Hilton, who have reproduced a refined Westernness in the decor, food and service of their hotels worldwide.

There are practical considerations, too. Parents traveling with young children will want to take nappies (diapers) and wet wipes, loads of (noncarbonated) drinks, and books and anything else that will keep their little ones occupied. Again, several airlines provide their own "keep busy" kits for younger passengers (*see* **Children**).

Elderly passengers with cardiovascular and respiratory problems should consider ordering supplemental oxygen from the airline 48 hours before departure (*see* **Supplemental Oxygen**). Advance notice should also be given by passengers who require special meals on board (*see* **Meals**).

Businesspeople must be selective about the sort of work they take in-flight, as the flight environment reduces your level of concentration and limits your ability to take in new or complex information (*see* **Oxygen Deficiency**). It is best to stick to simple routine work or something creative such as writing a speech.

Passengers who may be predisposed either to air sickness or apprehension may want to opt for a window seat. Digby Mackworth, a pilot with *British Airways*, suggests this solution because these symptoms can be caused by disorientation due to the maneuvring of the aircraft. Being able to see out of the window may help passengers to allay their fears about the movements of the aircraft.

PREPARING FOR TAKE-OFF There are several things you can do to prepare your mind and body for air travel.

TIME ZONES International travelers have to contend with unfamiliar cultures as well as with changes in climate and time zones. Of these factors, the one that is most difficult to adjust to is the time change. You can always pick up a few words of a new language or find out about cultural differences, pack the right clothes and have the appropriate immunizations and medicines. But how do you cope with a new time? The short answer is sleep and food (*see* **Sleep** and **Jetlag**).

If you cannot sleep on board the aircraft and need to be awake at your destination I can recommend an unusual method which does not involve stimulants such as coffee or tobacco: Limit your food intake. Not only is it easier to stay awake on an empty stomach, but eating less increases your level of concentration. Aviators including Charles Lindbergh and Wiley Post used this method to good effect on their pioneering journeys. Lindbergh ate just one sandwich in the course of his first 34-hour transatlantic flight.

EXERCISE Anyone who goes on an international flight has to face the fact that he or she is going to be inactive for long periods of time. Exercise is an essential feature of pre-flight planning as it helps to offset the effects on your body (particularly on circulation) of the reduced air pressure on board.

Swimming is the best and can be undertaken by anyone irrespective of fitness. Hotels at or near airports usually have swimming pools, making it more convenient to have a swim before departure. Some hotels, such as the Ritz-Carlton, facilitate this by providing their guests with disposable swimwear. It is never too late to exercise, even at the departure gate. Sitting immobile for hours pre-flight is a bad strategy. Of all passengers, frequent flyers in particular should ensure that they always exercise regularly before and after a flight (*see* **Exercise**).

PSYCHOLOGY There are three techniques that can be useful for preparing yourself psychologically for your flight. The first is to carry out a ritual of familiarization, which involves doing similar things throughout each journey (always traveling with the same airline, getting the same seat number and staying in the same hotel, for example). The second, according to frequent flyer Roger Goldman, a banker at National Westminster Bancorp, is to adjust mentally to the length of the flight you are undertaking: "on 14-hour flights," he says, "act as if you are never going to get off the aircraft. For an eight-hour journey, pretend you are going to the nether world, while for three to six hours tell yourself it will be over before you know it."

The third is to plan a treat for yourself if, as Jim Fifield, president of EMI Music says, you find long-haul trips problematic. "I plan stopovers particularly on flights from New York to Japan or Australia," he points out. "For example, in Honolulu where I can swim in the ocean and I don't even lose a day because of the international date line. It's definitely a psychological plus."

AIRPORTS Airports can be stressful. Therefore it is important to limit your exposure to stress (*see* **Stress**).

If you are an eager beaver, this is the moment to catch up on the paperwork you've got in your hold-all. This is an ideal way to deal with delays, too. "If there is one thing I've learned about air travel," says Jack Freeman of Unilever, "it is to practice patience." Some businesspeople take their secretaries to the airport to brief them on last-minute arrangements. Others arrange meetings in the airline's lounge. Should anything crop up later in the air, however, Singapore Airlines has introduced global phone and fax facilities on board.

Passengers on night flights should plan to have dinner at the airport and sleep on board. Some people may wish to prepare themselves for sleep by spending an hour or so window shopping (*see* **Sleep**).

IN-FLIGHT

By now you should have changed into your casual clothes, if you are not wearing them already. Don't forget warm clothing such as a pullover or cardigan. As a matter of course, limit your intake of food to three meals every 24 hours. Skipping a meal is far better than having an extra one. Some passengers pick at their food on board, as they find this helps to reduce jetlag. Remember, too, to eat a banana just before landing.

Once you have settled in your seat, carry out the different strategies that enhance your "safe space" (*see* **Safe Space**). Drink your **Wonder Juice** if you have not already done so, and keep yourself topped up with water. Ensure that you use the relevant items in your in-flight health kit. Swallow your aspirin to help your blood's anticoagulation factor, and rub on your various moisturizing gels two or three times during the flight. An essential article for me is the nasal and sinus refresher made by Danièle Ryman, which protects me from other people's ills and keeps my nose uncongested. Tea tree, lavender, eucalyptus or pine essential oils could also be used.

On board, the best state of mind to be in is one of repose—or even better, sleep. In such an instance the earplugs and eye mask are useful. Watch the movie if it is a comedy or family entertainment. Avoid anything that is violent or disturbing. Exercise in your seat, *not* in the aisles, as strenuous exercise is counterproductive because of the slight oxygen deficiency on board. I know of a passenger who just listens to his workout tape on a walkman—he swears that this gets him into a sweat! Before you land, apply a cooling eye compress to reduce facial puffiness.

Six-Million Miler

✈ Wallace Hawkes, who is the first six-million miler for *Delta Air Lines*, has flown the equivalent of 12 round trips to the moon. But as he has only been clocked by the airline for the past 13 years of his 35-year career, the total mileage is likely to be nearer 16 million miles.

He is an executive vice-president of an engineering company, Greiner Inc. based in Tampa, Florida, and supervises the construction of bridges, airports and highways around the world. As a result, he is in the air some four days a week and flies to Asia once a month. Recently, he has averaged 100,000 miles a month.

Like most business flyers, he works late and boards the night flight. "I can't afford to spend all day flying," he says. "I left Tampa last night for a meeting in Seattle this morning and tonight I'll be in Carson City."

Over the years, he has developed his own well-being program. He never sits at a window seat or checks in luggage and rarely eats airline food. "I've seen the tops of enough clouds to last the rest of my life," he comments. He carries on board the same small wheeled suitcase favored by airline staff. Among its contents are business folders, a computerized calendar and address book, the latest copy of the *Official Airline Guide* and a tiny cellular phone that enables him to call anywhere in the world.

"I travel light because by the time the bags come up, I'm already at the hotel."

He eschews food in-flight and is satisfied with an airport pizza on arrival. But if he is on a double red-eye flight, such as to Hong Kong, he will snack on sugar cookies, fruit or cheese about 10 hours into the 16-hour journey. To relax on board he will sometimes drink a glass of white wine mixed with club soda. Although his health is good and his weight has been constant over the past 15 years, he admits to having a sensitive stomach. As he is always on such a tight schedule he has a backup plan to avoid frustration en route. "If I see there's a problem," he says, "I don't wait around for them to admit it and then have to stand in line with 200 other people. I go for the alternative flight and make sure I'm on it." Once on board, he sleeps; even if he can't get to sleep he never takes sleeping pills. "They mess up your system," he states.

POST-FLIGHT

You have just landed. Why not clap as many passengers do, instead of ignoring the event? Such a response can help to release tension and express your joy of flying (and arriving)! Derek McMahon of Shell observes that out of a sense of relief after an uneventful flight we all stand up immediately in spite of knowing that it will take another 10-15 minutes before we can disembark. This is not done when we reach our destination by surface transport such as a train or bus.

Soon you will be able to reap the benefits of flying healthy. But there are still a few details that must be attended to before your plan is complete. These involve the local time, eating and exercising.

If there is anything that should be adhered to once you are back on terra firma, it is local time. Daylight and darkness are strong "resynchronizers." Therefore, stick to the local time as much as you can. There are some passengers whose body clocks are already synchronized because of the sleep they got during the flight. Others, who have not managed to sleep on board but who have relaxed, should expose themselves to the daylight and stay up for as long as they can. On the other hand, if it is night, go to bed—but again, as late as you can (around midnight).

Another strong synchronizer is food. If you have been abstemious during the flight you can now have a meal either at the airport or after you have checked in at your hotel. The type of food you eat is important: Avoid hamburgers and chocolate bars. Go for complex carbohydrates such as granola/muesli bars, sandwiches, pasta, rice or potatoes. For dessert eat a yogurt with a live bacterial culture. On the other hand, if your stomach is unsettled after a flight a natural yogurt might do the trick. Take supplements of vitamins E and C to counteract the effects of any free radicals (resulting from cosmic rays) you may have been exposed to during the flight. Continue the dosage for a couple of weeks after your flight.

Passengers who suffer from constipation may like to try kiwifruit, which has laxative properties. The regular working of one's bowels, together with a normal eating and sleeping pattern, help to adjust your body clock to local time more quickly.

Exercising after you arrive oxygenates your body, which has been short of oxygen on board. You may wish to exercise before your meal. Sir Sydney Lipworth Q.C. exercises immediately after a flight. He either sweats out the toxins in a game of tennis or in a brisk walk.

The author and foreign correspondent Ryszard Kupuscinski deliberately keeps his hotel room in something of a mess. He feels more at home if his possessions are all around him, imposing his identity on an otherwise sterile hotel suite and creating a "safe space" where he can relax and concentrate. So once you have unpacked, you might want to leave some of your things out where you can see them and be comforted by them.

To refresh or relax, I take a bath with aromatherapy essences such as Danièle Ryman's *Awake* or *Asleep* fragrances. *Awake* contains several stimulating aromas such as ylang ylang, while *Asleep* has tranquillizing ones. A mixture of stimulating essential oils and a combination of relaxing essential oils could also be used instead.

These can help your biological rhythms adjust to local time by encouraging either sleep or alertness. Some cabin crews take an aspirin before they go to bed as they find this helps them sleep better. Karen Goebel, an experienced purser on *Lufthansa*, has a perfect nightcap. She mixes a dry martini with the juice of two lemons as it settles her stomach and enables her to sleep soundly.

In all, if your body is in good shape after the flight you will quickly get into local sleeping and eating patterns. This will make you more confident and positive about flying, so that each journey is more enjoyable than the last.

Two

A–Z OF AVIATION HEALTH

AEROPHOBIA (FEAR OF FLYING)

On the plane trip out, I consider the meaning
of life to overcome my fear of flying.
I wonder if it's a laboratory and I'm
just another guinea pig. In the vast
scheme of things. As it were.
JULIA PHILLIPS, AUTHOR AND MOVIE PRODUCER

Aerophobia, or fear of flying, is an anxiety unlike other phobias because it can recur even after supposedly successful treatment. However, there is a great distinction to be made between other anxiety disorders and the nervousness that most passengers experience when they fly. The attitude of aerophobics—dubbed "white-knuckle flyers" because of their manner of clutching the armrests of their seats during take-off—is caused mainly by their lack of knowledge about the relative safety of flying. Sufferers will undoubtedly benefit from this book, particularly this entry, the one on **Aviation Psychology** and the last section, "Enjoy Your Flight!"

This phobia is complex, which goes some way toward explaining its unusual feature of recurring. It stems from several different types of distorted thinking. There are six elements of aerophobia that have been distinguished:

- claustrophobia, in which a person feels trapped and fears suffocation
- a panic-related anxiety in which the subject fears that he or she may experience a heart attack, go crazy or lose control yet have no means of escaping the aircraft
- space phobia, whereby a person is terrified by the idea of being "surrounded by nothingness"
- the fear of the aircraft crashing because of adverse weather, mechanical failure or a terrorist bomb
- the fear of heights
- post-traumatic reaction in which the fear of flying follows an emergency landing or ear problems.

Most studies demonstrate that anxiety disorders such as this are more predominant in the middle-aged than in the young or elderly, and more common among women than men. *Lufthansa*, one of the first airlines to offer seminars for passengers on relaxed flying, has come to similar conclusions. Since 1981 the airline's seminars have had over 4,000 participants whose average age has been 41 years. Of these, 52 percent were women and 71 percent had flown previously. The types of fears expressed by these passengers vary widely according to Barbara Fose, a psychologist on *Lufthansa*'s seminars.

One woman's fear appeared to stem from claustrophobia as she could not be in a room in which the door was closed. After the seminar, however, her problem with closed doors disappeared. Another woman who was in her late sixties believed that it was "against God's wishes" for people to fly. But as she wanted to see her daughter and grandchildren who lived in the U.S., she took part in the seminar. Gradually she, too, overcame her misgivings and was able to fly successfully. Another participant was a 16-year-old boy, who in spite of being a regular flyer suddenly showed symptoms of aversion. He would cry at the sight of an aircraft and once on board would experience breathing difficulties. The problem proved to be at heart a form of rebellion against his parents, who expected him to visit them in Ibiza every weekend rather than stay with his friends in Frankfurt. A famous German actor was also a participant. "People are only numbers in a plane," he said, expressing his fear of insignificance. "Decisions are made by unknown men—or nowadays even women!" Eventually his feelings of powerlessness (not to mention sexism!) were overcome and he found he could quite happily become "one of the many" aboard an international flight.

Although several airlines besides *Lufthansa*, such as *British Airways, American Airlines, Austrian Airlines, Swissair, SAS* and *KLM* also offer seminars on relaxed flying and have had long-term success rates for their graduates (in the case of *Lufthansa* as high as 90 percent), there remains little real knowledge about the flying phobia.

The type of treatment practised by most airlines is

based on behavioral concepts such as desensitization. Here the participants' fear is gradually overcome through repeated confrontation of the object or situation.

Another technique is the cognitive approach, whereby passengers are encouraged to change the way in which they process information and beliefs about flying. This approach works well with flight attendants. Randy Chauvin, who is responsible for some programs for *Delta Air Lines* involving the motion-based aircraft simulator, has noticed changes in the attitudes of the flight attendants who participate:

> They start off with a fear of flying which is mostly due to a lack of knowledge. Once they become familiar with emergency procedures, their fears are alleviated. They have gained confidence in as much as they know they have a chance in the worst scenarios. This positive approach is passed on to passengers should an emergency occur.

An American guest at the Mandarin Hotel in Hong Kong, who hated flying on her own, requested that the concierge purchase a huge teddy bear so that it could sit in the seat next to her and she could feel secure.

Doris Day, whose greatest fear is aerophobia, was asked in what form she would like to come back to this earth. Her reply was as a bird. "I always thought it would be wonderful to fly, but not in an airplane," she said.

Various options are available to treat aerophobia:

1. Most airlines run courses for fearful flyers.
2. The medical profession provides psychotherapy

    through chartered clinical psychologists (U.K.) and cognitive behavioural therapists (U.S.).

3. Stress therapy, such as Transcendental Meditation (TM), is a useful alternative to clinical intervention.

4. Confronting your fear directly often works, even if that means over-compensating for it. Learning to fly an aircraft yourself, for example, as in the case of the industrialist Sir Philip Beck, or overcoming your fear of heights by mountain climbing are two tried-and-tested methods.

5. Those who like to feel more in control of the situation may benefit from trying out a simulator, in which they can experience "piloting" an aircraft for themselves. *British Airways* offers such an opportunity for around £300 ($450) an hour (see last chapter, "Enjoy Your Flight!").

6. As a frequent shorthaul flyer, Jack Freeman of Unilever suffered severely from claustrophobia. He would even lie awake at night thinking about the small space in the aircraft he would have to face the next day. His novel solution was to look at the thighs of the flight attendants during the flight and his condition disappeared. He displaced his anxiety through sexual arousal (see **Sex**).

A Novel Cure

✈ Michael Edwards, a veteran car collector from Oxford and proud owner of the earliest surviving Hotchkiss 1904, overcame his fear of flying in a way any of us could emulate:

I learned to fly a Chipmunk at the age of 17. One day as I was on my way to my lesson I found that the Chipmunk had dug a garden in the left-hand lane of the motorway near the airport. It had nose-dived into the tarmac. I turned around and went home, and from then on I was afraid of flying.

But over the past two decades I have managed to overcome my apprehension. I hoard books or articles that I'm dying to read for the occasion when I have to fly. One of the books I'm going to read on my next flight is The Amateur Motorist *by* Max Pemberton, *which was published in 1908.*

As soon as I am on board I fasten my seat belt and take out my book or magazine. The most anxious moment is while the plane is on the runway as it takes off. By that time I am very involved in my reading. During the flight, my preoccupation is so complete that when I next notice, the plane has landed.

AIRLINE SEATS

The peculiar tilt of some airline seats (35 degrees) is a well-known angle used by interrogators to deprive their subjects of sleep.
DR. ANN SHARPLEY, MEDICAL RESEARCH COUNCIL
UNIT AND SLEEP LABORATORY, OXFORD

Airline seats is a topic which, like the English weather, produces countless criticisms. Although this piece of aircraft furniture is the end result of many considerations including cost, ergonomics, health and safety, none is so contentious as comfort. A simple definition is not difficult: comfort for most people is a seat that is soft to sit on because it yields to the weight of the body.

The prime concern of airlines is that their seats fit specific configurations that may be changed according to the airline's individual needs. Although there are three types of seats available in terms of comfort, it is best to distinguish between only two: those in Economy and those in the Premium Classes (Business and First). There is a world of difference between the two, as reflected in the price: an airline may pay $1,050 for an Economy seat, while up to $9,000 can be spent on one for First Class. In addition, there could be extra costs of some $4,500 for personalized video systems, etc., that go with the latter.

The significance of the seat and the space and comfort it affords, particularly on long-haul flights, is recognized by both the manufacturers and airlines. It is the single most important feature of the in-flight product for the majority of First and Business Class passengers, who in some cases generate 50 percent or more of airline revenue. Sometimes seat comfort is the sole reason for passengers' choice of one airline over another. Consequently, whether the passengers want to relax, work, eat, sleep or be entertained, their seats must provide their most satisfying environment. Whereas with Economy passengers, it is assumed that their prime consideration is thrift rather than comfort.

In ergonomic terms, there are two factors that have to be considered, for both classes. Due to limited space, the seat has to incorporate a meal table. It must also provide its occupant with sufficient lumbar support to ease the stress on the back and legs caused by long periods spent sitting down.

Where the two types of seats diverge is in their ability to recline. With Premium Classes, the backrest, footrest and in some cases even the headrest are adjustable to satisfy the individual comfort requirements of passengers. This is a physiological bonus, for it places the body in the position that encourages both sleep and circulation (*see* **Blood Circulation**).

Of the various elements that are incorporated into the seat, the least obvious are safety measures. However, for international civil aviation authorities (and many passengers) this is its most important function. As a result, seats are usually made from a tubular steel frame in double, triple or quadruple units that are strong enough to withstand the strain of severe air turbulence or an emergency impact. The force this represents is an acceleration nine times that of gravity ($9G$) forward and $1.5-4.5G$ rearward, sideways, upwards and downwards.

One frequent flyer who has definite opinions about seat comfort is Sir Norman Foster, the top international architect who has since 1964 won innumerable awards for his designs. As he spends 100,000 miles per annum in the air he is also conversant with a variety of Premium Class seats. "They don't recline enough for sleeping," he says, "and I usually end up propping up the leg-rest with my briefcase to gain greater height."

He suggests that the first airline to turn the clock back to the period of "flying boats," which provided proper sleeping compartments, would make a fortune. For him the problem revolves around design. The manufacturers, he advises, should "think of a bed converted to a seat rather than a seat converted to a bed."

Gore Vidal, author, recalls a memorable overnight flight from New York to Rome in the late fifties when he slept well. "There were, in those gracious times, overhead beds that came down when one wanted to sleep, rather like Pullman trains of long ago. Hard to imagine that commercial flying could ever have been pleasurable." Since this requirement was first mentioned in the U.K. edition of this book, two airlines have decided to reintroduce seats that turn into beds, i.e., *British Airways* and *Air France*.

HOW TO BE COMFORTABLE IN ECONOMY OR TOURIST SEATS

In a classic experiment conducted by an airline seat manufacturer, several people sat in different positions in sand. It was found that a person could occupy a small space yet still be comfortable. The key was to spread the body's weight around. People who sit in public places, such as hotel lounges, tend to re-enact this scenario automatically, moving their limbs about in unusual positions to achieve comfort. Instead of sitting erect in a seat and concentrating all their weight on the buttocks, they distribute it to various parts of the body.

This can be achieved in an airline seat as follows:

1. The head, which weighs at least 15 pounds, should be cradled in the hand or rested on an inflatable pillow.
2. The heaviness of the torso should be displaced by placing a pillow behind the small of the back. This angle allows it to lean more against the backrest. Tilting the backrest is also helpful.

3. The legs should be elevated from the floor, either by placing the feet on hand luggage or by inserting a pillow between the thighs and bottom part of the seat. The ideal angle from the back to the edge of the seat is 11 degrees.

4. For sick or disabled passengers, some airlines (such as *Swissair*) provide special seats with adjustable leg supports which can be positioned to provide the most comfort. Their aircraft also carry collapsible wheelchairs of the same height as other seats (these can be pre-booked in advance as necessary). At airports, wheelchairs are standard equipment for *Swissair* and some other airlines.

As a result of these measures, the different parts of the body can "lay their burden down" and the comfort factor will increase. All you need to do now is don your eye shades and insert your earplugs—you may even fall asleep!

ALCOHOL

One in the air is equivalent to two on the ground.
A WELL-KNOWN ADAGE AMONG AIRLINE CREWS

Most passengers are unaware that the cabin environment increases the effects of alcohol on the body (*see* **Medications**).

It has been demonstrated in experiments that drinking two or three cocktails while airborne has the physiological effect of four or five drunk on terra firma.

Alcohol's principal action is to slow down brain activity by restricting oxygen intake to the brain. When passengers ascend to moderate altitudes while on a plane they are already subjected to the additional oxygen deficiency caused by lower pressure in the cabin. This "double-whammy" makes alcohol have a much more powerful effect than normal.

Some air travelers who are more vulnerable than others to the concentration of alcohol in their bloodstream find that the consumption of only a couple of drinks can produce an "instant hangover" that lasts the duration of the flight.

Using alcohol to induce sleep on board may also backfire. Although sleep is promoted by alcohol because of its sedative effect, if more than a specified amount is drunk it can cause insomnia. Passengers who are used to an alcoholic nightcap of brandy or whisky may accordingly want to reduce their intake to half a glass of either, or to switch to a glass of wine.

As alcohol has a different potency in the air you may wish to limit your intake during the flight (see Table 1 in Appendix A).

1. Drink wine rather than spirits as a glass of wine has far fewer units than a glass of spirits. Beer, too, has less units than spirits but is not recommended because of its gaseous content (see **Gas Expansion**). Cocktails (such as a Bloody Mary or Martini) have the least number of units per glass.
2. If you do drink alcohol, make sure it is only when accompanied by a meal.
3. A drink *before* take-off may be a good solution because it will not only relax you but reduce stress. A glass of

champagne, which is a "euphoric," is an excellent way to begin a flight.

AMENITY KITS

Amenity kits originated in the 1930s when chewing gum, a phial of ammonia and cotton wool balls were standard issue for most air travelers.

The first helped to ease the effects of pressure changes in the air on your ears, the second was inhaled at the initial stages of airsickness and the last screened out noise in the cabin, which was not soundproofed at that time. Today, the amenity kit is a useful accoutrement which is usually provided free in Premium Class. The only exception is on *Concorde*, where a special gift is given to every passenger.

One of the most popular items among business flyers is a rehydration gel, as provided by *British Airways* in their Club World Kit.

Some people never travel without torches (flashlights), herbal teabags to help them unwind (camomile) or to ease digestion (peppermint), alarm clocks or inflatable neck pillows. There is also a most unusual object for those who do not mind how they look on board and have a dislike of quaffing water on flights. It is called a "humidiflyer" which, when fitted, resembles a gas mask and has a device to prevent moisture loss through breathing. This is available from a company of the same name in Australia (*see* Appendix B). *Japanese*

Air Lines has a similar device, a honeycomb mask for preserving moisture that is part of its "Travel Assistance Bag" for Premium Class customers.

All in all, an amenity kit plays an essential role in preserving your **Safe Space** on board.

You can assemble your own amenity kit to suit your individual needs. The essential items can include:

- earplugs
- eye masks
- toothbrush and toothpaste
- mouthwash
- disposable razor.

The health-conscious will add things such as:

- facial sprays
- cooling eye compresses or eye drops
- moisturizers.

Flyer No. 1

✈ Benny Hart is one of the longest-serving flight attendants in the world. She has flown for 47 years, with only eight days off sick. The key to her good health has been her positive personality. She is described by her colleagues on *Delta Air Lines* as a charming person who is an inspiration to others.

Her first flight was on a DC-3 prop in 1947

which covered a distance of 240 miles from Atlanta to St. Simons, Georgia, while her last was across five time zones and some 4,500 miles from Hawaii to Atlanta on a Lockheed-1011.

Her advice for passengers is to go with the flow as the body will later regain its balance. "If you wake up at 6 A.M.," she says, "and want to eat a steak and eggs or ice-cream, indulge yourself. I always do." On long-haul flights she consumes only a can or two of cola and on arrival washes her face with soap and water before applying cold cream to deal with dry skin.

There are also aspects of air travel that she believes can be overcome by the right mental attitude. This applies to sleep and jetlag. "Passengers who want to sleep on board," she observes, "will sleep. Equally, you can will yourself not to suffer from the effects of crossing time zones. Problems usually arise when people force themselves to go on a flight when they don't want to go."

Above all, her main message is for air travelers to treat their trip as an adventure, not a challenge.

ASTHMA

Some 5 percent of passengers on flights from the U.S. and the U.K. may have asthma, and between 5 and 10 percent may have had asthma in the past.

Nevertheless, it is rare for acute asthmatic episodes to occur in the air, although factors such as how anxious the asthmatic passenger is and how stuffy the cabin is do come into play.

In general, air travelers with stable asthma tolerate the moderate oxygen deficiency of the pressurized cabin as long as adequate bronchodilator therapy (with or without corticosteroids) is used. On the other hand, severe chronic asthmatics should have a pre-flight evaluation before a long-haul trip to assess their arterial partial oxygen pressure (PAO2). Such a measurement remains a reliable test for predicting their ability to withstand the lower pressure in the cabin. If this is less than the required 70 mmHg, provision can be made for supplemental oxygen on the flight (*see* **Supplemental Oxygen**).

As a standard procedure, asthmatics should review their treatment prior to their departure and ensure that they have an adequate supply of routine as well as emergency medications for their journey. This should include antibiotics if the sufferer is prone to chest infections. In addition, they should have a good management plan in the event of their condition deteriorating unexpectedly. All their medication should be readily available in their hand luggage and they should arrange to have a seat well away from the smoking section.

Time zone changes, too, should be taken into account. Passengers with moderate to severe asthma should continue taking their medication at their usual home time. On arrival, the intervals between medications should be adjusted to the local time. For example, if traveling from London to New York, the asthmatic passenger would take his or her medicine at, say, 11 A.M. London time, 4 P.M. London time, then 3 P.M. New York time (8 P.M. London time), and so on.

Most major airlines are equipped to deal with asthmatic attacks as their medical kits contain appropriate drugs (see **Medical Kits**). Some have nebulizers on board, too, such as *Air New Zealand*, while other airlines such as *Cathay Pacific* and *Virgin* can arrange to carry them if given at least 24 hours' advance notice. If passengers have their own electric nebulizers they will not be able to use them on board because of the high-frequency 115V aircraft system. Oxygen is also on hand from portable canisters should they feel the need for it.

As a last resort, a diversion to the nearest airport can be arranged if necessary. This is costly for the airline, but such a decision is usually deferred to a doctor or physician (in 80 percent of cases there is usually at least one passenger on board who is a doctor).

Stress, which can sometimes precipitate an asthmatic attack, can be minimized on flights (see **Stress**).

AVIATION PSYCHOLOGY

"I always feel in a state of elation after flying," says Lady Sabiha Foster, a director of Sir Norman Foster and Partners. "It satisfies a desire to go above and beyond."

Aviation psychology, which enables pilots to understand new concepts of speed, movement, spatial orientation or disorientation and sensory perception, is unknown to passive flyers. Yet there are some passengers who are aware of this mental attitude and can tap into its benefits. The aerial environment is so unique that when we are airborne we must try to discard our terrestrial responses.

Landscapes in the distance appear to move in a strange manner and the viewer's senses fail to deliver the information needed—that is, where the viewer is and in which direction the plane is moving. The air rushing by is of course invisible and the two large vortexes that the wings of an aircraft create as a wake remain unseen. The pilot's eye is afforded no perspective and judgement of depth, and distance can only be interpreted by the brain through instruments. Speed is a kinesthetic experience, either heard as it hisses against the skin of the aircraft or felt through muscle tension and the position of the joints and tendons.

There is freedom of movement in an aircraft unknown on the earth and the pilot must learn to let go of the ground. He or she can put the aircraft through at least six kinds of motion at once: speeding forward, slipping sidewise, climbing or sinking, rolling over sidewise, pitching the plane's nose up or down and to the right or left.

Sometimes during training, when pilots have problems in the air, their instinct is to grab hold of something solid like the controls. This is a temporary reversion to earthbound psychology. There are stories from the early days of flying when instructors had to have a fire extinguisher handy, not for use on fires but to slug the student who had frozen at the controls. Once pilots get the hang of this new aviation psychology they gain a special "air sense" by which they know their way around the sky. They are no longer part of the landscape but of the wind that blows over it. Their experience of freedom is unknown on earth, for they have achieved the dream of flight.

Such an achievement produces an emotion of joy in active flyers that rarely palls even after decades of flying. Captain Jock Lowe, test pilot for *Concorde* 25 years ago, confesses that the SST still provides thrills, as it did on the first flight. "The only other pilots up there," he says, "are fighter pilots in pressure suits." Another view is provided by Geoffrey Mussett, captain of the *Concorde* fleet. "There's the excitement at take-off of having in your hands a piece of precision machinery— in fact, the first genuine piece of twenty-first-century technology. The aircraft does exactly what you want. It's absolutely smooth at speeds of between 1,300 and 1,400 mph."

Passengers who are bored or preoccupied with mundane thoughts such as the next intake of food and drink, and the movie to be screened, can change their attitude to air travel. There is a high level of energy on board which, according to acupuncturists, disturbs the body's flow as well as the balance between the meridians. These changes can be used to your benefit. Above all, we have momentarily cut the umbilical cord with the earth and are speeding along above the clouds. This idea is powerful enough to trigger in anyone a sense of exhilaration that can be harnessed creatively.

The film director Robert Altman was inspired to make the film *Short Cuts* after reading Raymond

Carver's short stories on a 12-hour flight from Italy to the U.S. "I started reading the stories and falling asleep and then waking up and reading a couple more, and then falling asleep again," he says. "By the time I got off the plane all the stories had kind of run together, and I had made 'Carver soup.' I thought, 'this is a movie!'"

Dr Gareth Carnaby, director of the Wool Research Organization at Lincoln University, New Zealand, had a similar experience on a flight from London to Japan. He invented a new spinning process that reduces the weight of an airline seat's fabric, resulting in savings for the airlines. "I had spent much of the flight trying to think of a way of spinning threads finer. The answer came to me finally when we were flying over Alaska."

Even on a short flight, creative new ways of thinking (the essence of aviation psychology) can be practiced. The painter Henri Matisse has provided an interesting insight into this:

A simple voyage by plane from Paris to London gives us a revelation of the world which our imagination cannot anticipate. At the same time that the feeling of our new situation delights us, it confuses us with the memory of the cares and annoyances with which we let ourselves be troubled on the same earth that we catch sight of below us, as we cross over holes in the plain of clouds that we are overlooking from an enchanted world, which was there all the time.

When we are returned to our modest condition of walking, we will no longer feel the weight of the grey sky upon us because we will remember that beyond this wall of clouds, so easily crossed, there exists the splendour of the sun; the perception of limitless space, in which we felt for a moment so free.

Next time you fly, think of the aircraft traveling in an ocean of air. You may not have a pilot's-eye-view but you can still share in the mastery of the skies. Put this extraterrestrial period to good use by experimenting with a new way of looking at your work or life. A distinguished mathematician from MIT and a centenarian, Professor Dirk Struik, advises passengers not to take themselves too seriously. He still flies regularly and although he is never troubled by jetlag, suffers from the occasional attack of boredom.

Elixir of Youth

✈ Woody Watkins, Purser on *American Airlines*, first started flying in 1968. There were few opportunities for flight attendants then, and she had to retire at 32 but returned when this rule was waived in 1974. Before she even starts her working day she has to commute 1,729 miles from her home in California to Chicago.

"It's a lifestyle, not a job," she insists. "I enjoy shopping, eating, walking in various cities as well as touring. Where else can you have a champagne appetite on a beer budget?" Travel, which she has always found to be intellectually stimulating, has also had a positive influence on other aspects of her life. She was encouraged to study for the U.S. Bar examinations and qualified as a lawyer. Her intention was to practice on her days off, but this has not worked out so far.

"Flying keeps me young," she says. "I'm usually taken to be several years younger than my contemporaries back in California."

BLOOD CIRCULATION

Modern transport has dramatically reduced the use of our legs and caused inadequate circulation in most people.

The total lack of movement in the cramped quarters of an aircraft for several hours results in the most common symptom of air travel: swollen feet, ankles or legs.

This sign of poor circulation soon disappears after arrival except in the elderly where it can persist for up to 48 hours. However, for a very small number of passengers there is an additional downside as they can develop what is known as the "Economy Class Syndrome" or Deep Vein Thrombosis (DVT). This can also occur on prolonged journeys in other forms of transport or just by remaining in a cramped position over a period of time. In some cases DVT can lead to pulmonary embolism. On a flight of three hours or more there is a potential risk of blood clots forming in the deep veins of the leg and the pelvis; these clots could later break free and lodge in an artery of the lung.

The reason for DVT is twofold: When seated, the pumping action of the calf and thigh muscles is no longer used to get the blood up to the heart. At the same time, the pressure of the edge of the seat blocks the return of the venous blood. Consequently, the flow of blood is halved and after a period it pools to form swollen feet and ankles.

Posture can affect our blood flow rate dramatically. In a standing or seated position it is halved. However, the flow rate is doubled while seated when the head is tipped downwards or after vigorous up and down movements of the feet to simulate walking (*see* **Exercise**). Contractions of the muscles in the feet and legs cause the veins to be "milked" and the blood forced upwards into larger veins and ultimately back to the heart. Michael Donne, who is 6 feet, 6½ inches tall, only travels Business Class on scheduled airlines as he has more space and can use the leg-rest.

Impaired circulation alone is not enough to produce a blood clot. Other factors come into play, including dehydration, the consumption of a fatty meal, and the use of oral contraceptives. Some passengers are also predisposed to the condition by virtue of cardiovascular disease which makes them prone to coagulation of the blood, or pregnancy, when the blood tends to be more viscous. Smokers too are at a higher-than-average risk of forming blood clots.

There are several simple methods that encourage good blood circulation while on board:

1. Keep your hand luggage on the floor in front of you, and rest your feet on it so that your thighs are clear off the edge of your seat. If this is not possible, resort to exercise. Short people should be particularly aware of the potential risk of blood-clotting, as they are more prone to pressure on their calves from the seat

than are their taller neighbors. Passengers over 6 feet tall, however, are also vulnerable because of the greater length of their veins, which makes it more difficult for the blood to flow back towards the heart.

2. If traveling in Business or First Class, keep your feet up on the leg-rest at the highest elevation. Check that there is no pressure on your calves.

3. Anticoagulants: aspirin or glyceryl guaiacolate. An aspirin can be taken the day before or during a long-haul flight. For short-haul flights you need only lick an aspirin to enjoy its benefits. A dose of two teaspoons of glyceryl guaiacolate is enough to help prevent blood clots.

4. Massage your calves several times during the flight with products such as Neal's Yard Comfrey and Mallow Foot Balm, Danièle Ryman's exercise gel or Clarin's Energising Emulsion. These will boost circulation.

5. Passengers with varicose veins should wear elastic or support stockings. This advice also applies to people who are overweight, on the pill or who have high blood pressure.

6. Walk briskly for at least half an hour before take-off (see **Exercise**).

A Vice President's Weakness

✈ Dan Quayle, former U.S. Vice President, was treated for blood clots in both his lungs and right leg which had been caused by prolonged sitting on an aircraft. He spent a week in hospital and was the prescribed six months of anticoagulant medication and restricted activity. His doctors at the Indiana University Medical Center insisted that he limit his schedule and forgo flying for at least six weeks.

CABIN AIR QUALITY

In the long term, filters on aircraft are being developed to supply recirculated air that is the microbial equivalent of fresh air.

Cabin air quality is a term that has not only been misunderstood by the public but misused by both airlines and aircraft manufacturers. The reason is that it is determined by a number of complex factors including ventilation, the use of fresh air or a mixture of fresh and recirculated air, contaminants, air filtration, cabin pressure and humidity (*see* **Humidity** and **Pressure Cabin**).

VENTILATION
Airflow begins with bled air from the engines which is already compressed and extremely hot. Most of the air is cooled in air-conditioning packs, but a small percentage of hot air is added to the cooler air to control the temperature within each cabin zone.

Recirculation fans increase cabin air ventilation and enable the air-conditioning packs to be operated at a reduced flow during the cruise of the aircraft. Such a system, using a mixture of fresh and circulated air, decreases the engine bleed requirements and in turn results in savings on fuel costs.

But to gain an understanding of cabin air quality, which is an essential element of a passenger's health, we have to examine the variables involved in the complex formation of ventilation. These include the design of the system, the presence and concentrations of contaminants and the filtration equipment.

For purposes of ventilation, the fuselage is divided into two main areas: the passenger cabin and the flight deck. The total volume of air, which in a 747–400 can amount to 11,040 cubic feet per minute (CFM), is exchanged, according to Boeing, every two to three minutes. However, in practice airlines indicate that this occurs every five minutes (and in the 767–300, for example, every six minutes).

In both these models, as indeed in all new aircraft, the ventilation consists of about 50 percent fresh (conditioned) air and 50 percent recirculated air. All recirculated air is cleared of pollutants in a filtration system that cannot be bypassed. (In earlier generations of aircraft such as the 727, 737-200 and *Concorde*, the equipment produces 100 percent fresh air.) (*See* Table 2 in Appendix A.)

What is not generally known is that the flow rate per person varies according to where you sit on the aircraft. If you happen to be Captain or First Officer, you could receive 120 CFM and upwards; in First and Business Class the rate is reduced to 40–60 CFM, while in the Economy Class the rate is reduced even further to 20 CFM per person. The reason for this disparity is that the seating density is highest in Economy Class. Obviously, if the seat configuration is changed to all Economy, the airflow per passenger can drop even further. The greater ventilation rate in the flight deck takes into account the specialized conditions in that area, which include night heat loss through the windows and skin of the aircraft, and the cooling necessary for the electrical equipment.

The current ventilation standards on the ground differ to a degree with those on board. The two leading engineering societies, ASHRAE and the Building Officials and Code Administrators (BOCA) recommend a minimum amount of 20 CFM of fresh air per person in buildings.

SOURCES OF CONTAMINANTS

The sources of contaminants in aircraft are similar to those found on the ground, with the exception of ozone.

Carbon Dioxide

The predominant source is carbon dioxide (CO_2), which is the product of exhalation and of the dry ice used in aircraft galleys. The concentration of CO_2 varies in the cabin according to the number of passengers present, their individual rates of CO_2 production and the fresh air rate. As a consequence, CO_2 has been used as an indicator of the overall efficiency of ventilation—that is, of indoor air quality. An excess reveals poor air quality.

Microorganisms

Microbial aerosols, which emanate from passengers and food, constitute the second largest group of contaminants in the cabin air. These microorganisms include bacteria, viruses, fungi such as molds, rust and yeast, and spores of either robust bacteria or fungi.

There are two ways in which these microorganisms become airborne: as a result of passengers sneezing, coughing, yawning or talking, and by means of dust particles generated from clothing, seating and soft furnishings such as the plane's curtains and carpets.

The movement of people around the cabin promotes ventilation but also keeps dust particles airborne. In general the movement of air helps to decrease infection. When a passenger coughs (which produces about 100,000 microscopic droplets), the droplets would be targeted at the nearest person if not for the presence of airflow, which will move the droplets toward the back of the aircraft and through the outflow valve.

With a very high efficiency filtration system and high recirculation rates the microorganisms are carried away from passengers and removed by filter membranes. As the air is continually being cleaned, passengers breathe air which is as free from contamination as possible.

ETS

Of all the contaminants, environmental tobacco smoke (ETS) is the only visible one and the cause of most complaints by passengers and aircrew. Indeed, ETS was the main reason why in 1986 the American Association of Flight Attendants brought the issue of Airliner Cabin Air Quality to the attention of the U.S. Congress and the public. This has resulted in a gradual worldwide ban on smoking on commercial (mainly domestic) flights. Two airlines, *Air Canada* and *Cathay Pacific*, have won World Health Organization (WHO) medals for providing smoke-free flights on the majority of their long-haul routes.

ETS is a complex mixture of gas and particulate contaminants composed of thousands of compounds. Most people are aware of its effects—which on one level can cause an irritation to the eyes, nose or throat, and on another cancer from the carcinogens that it contains. An aspect of ETS, which most passengers are unaware of, is the significant levels of carbon monoxide (CO) present. This CO combines with hemoglobin in the blood to reduce available blood oxygen as well as reducing the intake of oxygen. There is a tendency to become more hypoxic (suffer from lack of oxygen) as a result, and this blockage of oxygen by CO persists for up to five hours after exposure to cigarette smoke.

Some 4 to 8 percent of the haemoglobin is locked up with CO in cigarette smokers; passive smokers are also subjected to high levels of ETS when airborne.

In a survey carried out by *Swissair* to evaluate complaints on air quality, ETS was singled out as the top pollutant for both passengers and cabin crew.

These complaints were generated by a report of *symptoms* rather than specific contaminants. This can sometimes be misleading as, for example, the symptoms brought on by too much CO_2 can also arise if a cabin is too warm. *Swissair* has also commented on the fact that passengers and crew traveling in cooler cabins made fewer or no complaints (*see* Table 3 in Appendix A).

OZONE

Ozone (O_3), which is produced by the action of ultraviolet light on oxygen, is found mainly at high altitudes. On the ground the concentration of the gas is about 0.03 parts per million by volume (ppmv), rising to some 4 ppmv at 60,000 feet and about 10 ppmv at 100,000 feet. It is a powerful oxidizing agent and its toxic effects are primarily respiratory. Cabin ozone limits are set by the Federal Aviation Administration (FAA) Code of Federal Regulations, which confines ozone concentration to a maximum of 0.25 ppmv at any time above 32,000 feet. In addition, it may not exceed the maximum of 0.1 ppmv on three-hour flights.

There are at least three efficient methods of removing O_3. In the case of *Concorde*, the temperature reached by its air-conditioning compressor circuit is the same at which the gas decomposes into O_2 (oxygen). Therefore, this compressor circuit serves as a filter. The other two filters include the familiar platinum-based catalytic converter and an absorbent impregnated with an oxidizing agent. As the concentrations of O_3 are usually below FAA limits, most airlines do not install special equipment to remove the gas.

AIR FILTRATION

Increased energy costs have shifted the balance between the use of fresh outside air (which requires air conditioning) and the reuse of inexpensive indoor air. Consequently, there is a trend toward recirculation of cabin air which has placed greater emphasis on contamination control than in the past.

The need for filtration of cabin air fine enough to control contamination and remove harmful bacteria and viruses is met through high efficiency filters. Although the interaction between the contaminants is based on a relatively simple technique which originated in the mid-19th century, major advances in contamination control have recently been applied to aircraft cabins.

Contaminants and Control

Airborne contaminants in cabin air not only range in size but in form, and can either be gases or separate particles in a substance called *particulate* (*see* Table 4 in Appendix A). A simple illustration of the relative sizes involved is to use the diameter of a hair (75 micrometres) as a marker. The average bacterium measures 1 micrometer in diameter, viruses 0.01 micrometers, and gaseous molecules between 0.001 and 0.005 micrometers.

In terms of contamination control, there is an essential difference between gases and particulate. Filtration can remove particulate. The filter mechanism is described either as *Penetration* (based on the percentage of material passing through the filters) or *Efficiency* (based on the percentage of material retained by the filters). Gaseous pollutants, on the other hand, become attached to adsorbent material such as activated carbon and/or are converted into an innocuous substance—for example turning ozone into oxygen through the use of a platinum catalytic converter.

Airframe makers such as Boeing and Airbus fit their aircraft with High Efficiency Particulate Air (HEPA) Filters, which have minimum efficiencies of between 91 and 99 percent. These HEPA filters are able to remove particles as small as viruses as well as larger ones of up to 10 micrometres, such as those that comprise tobacco smoke and bacteria. The filter's efficiency increases over time but drops when the particulates approach the size of gas molecules. In computer models developed by the Pall Corporation, which evaluate the efficacy of such filtrations in aircraft cabins, it was found that because of the 50 percent fresh air content even systems with lower filter efficiency will eventually clean up contaminants. A filter with an efficiency of 99 percent and more will block pathological microorganisms at the first pass within three minutes, whereas a less efficient one could take up to half an hour to do the same job.

At present, the Boeing 747–400 is fitted with a HEPA filter that has a 95.9 percent efficiency, while some Airbus models have filters that operate at 97 percent efficiency. However, new aircraft such as the 777 and A330 will upgrade to 99.97 percent.

With the evolution of fuel-efficient planes, cabin air filtration systems will continue in the long term toward less fresh and more recirculated air (*see* Table 5 in Appendix A). At the same time, filters are being developed to reduce the penetration of contaminant particles by 50 to 500 times more than conventional cabin air filters, and to supply recirculated air that is the microbial equivalent of fresh air.

Healthy Flying

✈ Makram Zaccour, the vice chairman of the International Private Banking Group of Merrill Lynch, is an airline enthusiast and the most traveled of his colleagues.

He can recall flights taken in his youth such as a Christmas trip in a Dakota in 1949 from Beirut to Cairo, a journey in a Lockheed Constellation from Damascus to Geneva and an Easter holiday in 1951 when he flew in a three-engined JU52 Junker from Madrid to Seville. But the most memorable was a transatlantic crossing in another classic aircraft, the noisy Boeing Stratocruiser in which a bed or sleeperette was located in the overhead locker. (It took 14 hours but at least he slept well.)

One of his golden rules is to fly during the day and depart at the comfortable hour of 10 A.M. This ensures that his sleep pattern is not disrupted. "I prefer to sleep at the destination rather than on the aircraft," he explains. On occasions he has to fly at night, he orders a vegetarian meal so he can circumvent the lengthy meal service and retire immediately after take-off.

On board, he usually sits in seats that have the most space around them like those near bulkheads or the fire exits. Over the years he has found that this is a means of also ensuring that he does not catch other passengers' colds. Another cause of infections, he observes, is extreme changes in temperature; for example, when one flies from the northern to the hot southern hemisphere or from a cold to a warm climate. He gives as an illustration a trip to Latin America in the winter. It is his custom to leave his overcoat with the airline at Heathrow to make certain he can don it when he arrives back to windy, wet and cold weather.

There was a period in his life when he suffered from airsickness. "I'm very sensitive to movement as well as vibration on aircraft," he says. "But I found a cure—Dramamine tablets." However, after he was involved in a car accident he found that he was less affected as it appears that his sense of balance improved.

His briefcase always contains a V-neck sweater

in the upper pocket for use in the cabin and other essential items for travel, such as a spare pair of cufflinks, collar stiffeners, aspirin, Lemsip for colds and Dramamine. An important piece of clothing which he is seldom without is a Turnbull & Asser blazer for this can be matched with trousers from a gray winter suit or a summer beige suit.

Whenever he flies he invariably consults two thick volumes of the *ABC World Airways Guide*. They provide not only timetables and routes of the airlines but also the model of aircraft flown by an airline on a specific route. It is the latter that interests him because he always chooses the latest models to travel on. "I feel more comfortable in the newest aircraft," he explains.

CHILDREN

'Some babies bark like seals on long-haul flights," says Robert Hubbard of Delta Air Lines. "They tend to be out of sorts, crying a lot, and produce a dry cough which is the result of dehydration. The remedy is to get them to breathe oxygen through a moist hand towel."

Although children generally travel well, there are some points which parents should bear in mind.

Babies may suffer discomfort by pressure changes during aircraft descent: providing them with a bottle or dummy facilitates the equalization of pressure. Howling pitifully is another method of resolving the problem, but is of course a lot harder on the baby, his or her parents, and other passengers. Older children should be given chewing gum or boiled sweets (sucking candies).

An interest in flying is something that parents can encourage at an early age. John Munday is a nine-year-old who has flown to Los Angeles from London to visit his grandparents on 12 occasions since his birth. When he travels, he enjoys looking out of the window at the clouds and visiting the cockpit. As he really likes flying he has already had three flying lessons.

There is also a category of young flyers known by the airlines as unaccompanied minors (UMS). They hang out in a special executive lounge, the Sky Flyer, at Heathrow and are more assured than other children of the same age. On board, these young flyers roll their eyes throughout the safety demonstration, are experts with the seat controls and sometimes even try to order a Bloody Mary! But however blasé they appear to be, most are still accompanied by their favorite cuddly toy.

Some airlines make a special effort to entertain children when they fly. *Delta Air Lines*, which calls itself "the official airline for kids," has introduced a Fantastic Flyer program that features free activities and gifts to keep children from 2 to 12 occupied on board. There are over 700,000 members of the program from 150 countries; each member receives a Mickey Mouse visor with his or her application.

British Airways, too, is a parent-friendly airline which offers a children's service ranging from free nappies (diapers) to loaning "aunties" for UMS. Children's favorite radio and video programmes are available on flights, as well as goody bags for their amusement.

Innovative food for the young is also found on board (*see* **Meals**).

At Geneva and Zurich airports, there are play areas for children flying on *Swissair*, irrespective of the class of ticket they hold. During peak periods, special check-in desks are opened by the airline to accommodate families, and children are entertained by staff dressed up as the cartoon character Pingu the penguin. In common with some other airlines, *Swissair* offers families seat selection when they book and do all they can to make anyone traveling with children feel especially welcome.

As infants have a higher water content than adults (some 70 percent compared with 50–60 percent), they should be given small amounts of water at regular intervals during the trip. This will ensure that they do not become dehydrated. Children with bad colds or problem ears should not be taken on long-haul flights as they may be in great discomfort or even pain. The use of a decongestant may be helpful.

CONCORDE

It is pressurized at low cabin altitude and I'm unquestionably less tired as a result.
Sir Ronald Hampel, chairman of Imperial Chemical Industries (ICI) plc

In most people's minds *Concorde* is associated with speed, but few realize that it has another significant attribute: It is the world's healthiest aircraft.

As a supersonic transport (SST), it is exceptional

because it has the advantage over other (subsonic) aircraft in that human factors were given priority over economic and engineering considerations in its aeronautical design.

This led to an over-engineered pressure cabin to protect the occupants from the outside atmosphere (*see* **Pressure Cabin**). The safeguards incorporated into the design include substantial reserve air capacity to supply the cabin, the use of small windows (some six inches in diameter) and the low optimum cabin altitude. The plentiful air supply and small windows are essential in the instance of a decompression, which has never occurred in *Concorde*'s commercial service for either *British Airways* or *Air France*.

The low optimum cabin altitude enables the SST to fly high while at the same time maintaining a lower (5,000-foot) altitude in the cabin. This unique feature was attained at considerable economic sacrifice. The fuselage was reduced in size by 20 percent, with a corresponding loss in passenger revenue. Although the higher atmospheric pressure is of benefit to passengers as it reduces fatigue, it was introduced to meet specific demands of the flight deck after research at the RAF Institute of Aviation Medicine demonstrated that the ability to assimilate large inputs of information in novel or emergency situations could be impaired by even a slight lack of oxygen (or mild *hypoxia*). Both the flight crew and the passengers are thus at an advantage, because they breathe air as it would be at 5,000–6,000 feet rather than at the 8,000 feet which the long-range subsonics maintain as they fly.

There are other human factors that place the SST in the forefront. The aircraft uses a 100-percent fresh air flow system and therefore has no need for either recycling fans or cabin air filtration. The total volume of air, 7,063 cubic feet, is replaced every two and a half minutes and allows for each passenger to have 60 cubic feet per minute of fresh, clean air. As it has the best extraction unit for dispelling cigarette smoke there is little chance of passengers smelling environmental tobacco smoke.

The level of atmospheric ozone (O_3) has also been reduced radically as the aircraft has an efficient method of removing this gas, which is a respiratory irritant. This is achieved through the combination of a catalytic converter and exposing the O_3 to 400°C/752°F in the air-conditioning compressor circuit during ascent and cruise (ozone destabilizes to oxygen in hot temperatures). However, during descent when the temperature falls to 300°C/572°F for three minutes, the catalytic converter takes over the job of converting O_3 to O_2. Thus the SST is virtually ozone-free. Except for new models such as the Boeing 777, most conventional aircraft have no similar ozone-control equipment.

The main boon of supersonic travel is that passengers can maximize their air travel requirements with the minimum of mental and physical stress. There is the fast re-synchronization of biological rhythms thanks to the short flying time required to cover great distances. In the time it takes to fly from London to Athens or Philadelphia to New Orleans (some 3.5 hours), passengers have already crossed the Atlantic. The check-in time at *British Airways*, too, is streamlined so that travelers can arrive 20 minutes before departure. Whether a *Concorde* flight is taken from London or Paris to New York, the air travelers on arrival are ready to face the American experience at a considerable advantage to millions of other passengers.

"Regular travelers don't suffer from jetlag," Captain Dave Rowland, general manager *Concorde*, points out. "It is really a time-machine because you can leave London at 10.30 in the morning and arrive in New York at 9.20 A.M.!" There is also a story of a check that arrived too late to be accepted as cargo on the *Concorde*. The passenger offered to buy a ticket for it instead! The check was for $36 million and the passenger wanted it to be deposited in a New York bank at the beginning of the day's business, in order not to lose interest for that day (see page 80 for bargain flights on *Concorde*).

(More data on the SST appears in Table 6 in Appendix A.)

Blue Chip

✈ Sir Ronald Hampel is the Chairman of Imperial Chemical Industries (ICI) plc and has worked for the company since he graduated from Cambridge in 1955. He has worked for seven companies in the group and lived in four countries. "As the lifeblood of our business is research and technology," he says, "and the cost of bringing products to the market is high, we need to exploit it globally."

From 1966 onwards he has been involved in sales and has travelled internationally ever since. He has gone on a trip a week for at least three decades, including 100 flights on *Concorde*. "I unashamedly recommend it to save time as you can have a full day here in London and have dinner in New York."

In general his rule has been to listen to his body as it can adjust to various changes. Most of the time he ignores the clock at the destination and reacts rather to the needs of his body. "I don't force myself to sleep unless I'm tired," he comments. "Equally, when I go to New York and wake up at 5 A.M., I get up and work. The only issue that throws you out is when you're expected to work in the evening."

He has been around the world in a week on two occasions. The itinerary on the first trip included Philadelphia, London, Tokyo—on his return to Philadelphia he felt disorientated. That was the only time in his life when he was conscious of the negative effect of air travel. When he next went around the world in seven days, he slept on board, sometimes for 13 hours at a stretch, and was free of any symptoms.

As a frequent flyer he is fortunate in two respects: He is teetotal and has the ability to sleep anywhere. However, in spite of the latter, he still finds that he has to take sleeping tablets 10 percent of the time. On board he operates by a simple principle summarized in the acronym DAWN (Day flight–Aisle seat/Window seat–Night-flight). Having an aisle seat during a daytime flight enables him to move about more freely. However, the window seat is his preference during night-time travel as this keeps him from being disturbed by the meal service and no one needs to clamber over him. "I am sometimes asked why I don't travel less and make more use of satellite communications and video. Well, business is people-oriented and you need to meet them face to face."

DECOMPRESSION SICKNESS

Decompression sickness is characterized mainly by pains in the limbs. It can result either from a too rapid return to the surface after breathing under high pressure or from flying too soon following diving.

There is also the remote possibility of being in an aircraft which undergoes a slow or rapid decompression (*see* **Pressure Cabin**).

Decompression sickness is caused by the release of nitrogen bubbles in the blood and tissues. Poor solubility of the gas due to supersaturation arises when there is a lag between the rate of fall of the partial pressure of nitrogen in the body and the absolute pressure outside. This is triggered during a rapid ascent while underwater diving or while flying to an altitude of 18,000 feet and above in an unpressurized aircraft, and by the combination of diving and then flying soon afterwards.

Once the nitrogen bubbles are established they grow in size and are carried by the circulation to other parts of the body where they produce various symptoms, the most common being "the bends." Here, bubble formation occurs around and within a joint such as a knee, elbow, shoulder or wrist. A mild ache can progress to excruciating pain within 20 minutes to an hour on board.

Other less frequent symptoms include "the creeps" in which the bubbles are conveyed to the skin and produce a sensation of insects crawling on it, and "the chokes" whereby a person feels as if his or her chest is constricted and coughing is painful.

Decompression sickness is a serious condition and should be avoided at all costs. If you have been aqualung or scuba diving while on holiday, it is recommended that you allow several hours between your last dive and your departure time (the American Medical Association suggests an interval of 12 hours). If diving has taken you to a depth of 30 feet or more, allow at least 24 hours before air travel.

Where a flight is undertaken in a private aircraft, unpressurized, the use of supplemental oxygen is essential—or an immediate descent from 18,000 feet is advised. Passengers who in the future may be involved in a decompression incident on board an aircraft should take countermeasures as outlined in the entry on **Pressure Cabin**.

The treatment undertaken in a pressure chamber is only effective if it is carried out immediately. When cases of decompression sickness do occur, the person must be recompressed at once and decompressed gradually in accordance with the code of practice.

DIABETES

Although two to three passengers on board aircraft tend to have diabetes, some are too embarrassed to announce the fact.

As a result, it is not surprising to find that diabetes is in a list of seven of the most frequent in-flight medical problems (*see* **Medical Kits**). "Some typical incidents happen when passengers with diabetes drink alcohol, particularly white wine," says Robert Hubbard of *Delta*

Air Lines. "They become aggressive and demanding, only later to confess their condition."

There is no need for this to occur if passengers with diabetes plan well in advance of their trip. The difficulties that long-haul flights present include irregular meals, alcohol and insufficient exercise, resulting in inappropriate amounts of insulin and/or inappropriate snacks. This can give rise to hyperglycemia (where the blood sugar level is too high) and perhaps serious problems on arrival, or to hypoglycemia (a fall in blood sugar).

The medical kits of most major airlines do contain drugs to treat hypoglycemia in case this problem arises during a flight. However, it is important for passengers with diabetes to ensure that their medications have been packed in their hand luggage.

Passengers with diabetes who undertake journeys over several time zones should remain on home time throughout as regards meals and medication. This can be achieved with good planning through the cooperation of the airline or when the passengers include their own food together with their medications in their hand luggage.

An additional factor to consider in westward or eastward travel is that the insulin regimen will have to be adjusted slightly. For westward travel, the shift in time zones should be covered by one or two extra injections of short-acting insulin. The additional dose should be about 20 to 30 percent of the total daily dose. A decrease in dosage, by a similar amount, on eastbound flights maintains sound glycemic control. This is achieved by slightly reducing normal doses during the flight.

Keep well hydrated during the flight, as some people with diabetes can be prone to dizziness on board. A quick fix for a hypoglycemic passenger, according to a *Lufthansa* purser, Christine Behmer, is either a Coke or an apple juice because of their sugar content.

DIZZINESS AND FAINTING

> *"The "Coke fix" is the tried and tested method to prevent fainting on board,"* says Woody Watkins of American Airlines who has been flying since 1968. "As soon as passengers complain of being hot and giddy, I get a Coca-Cola down them as fast as possible."

The most common problem for passengers on long-haul flights (noted specifically in those seated at the rear of aircraft such as the Airbus 340 and Boeing 767) is dizzy spells, which usually result in fainting (*see* **Medical Kits**). This temporary loss of consciousness through deficient blood supply to the brain can occur after a meal and/or when a passenger rises after prolonged sitting. There are also instances of passengers who wake up after several hours of sleep to find that they feel hot and sweaty, who then faint as soon as they move around.

The digestion and absorption of food results in a rise of blood flow to the intestines, which is compensated by an increase in the heart rate. Consequently, blood-pressure and the flow of blood to the brain are not compromised. There are exceptions, however, such as in the case of elderly passengers and those with cardiovascular conditions or non-insulin dependent diabetes mellitus (*see* **Diabetes**). In these cases, eating may cause a fall in blood pressure and lead to feelings of dizziness, light-headedness and even to fainting. An additional factor which may have a bearing on the condition is the oxygen deficiency of the cabin, whereby a small drop in blood pressure may have a significant effect on cerebral function. Alcohol, too, raises the blood flow to the intestines and the heart rate.

According to Pat Evans, a flight attendant on *Virgin* Airlines, the majority of those affected are overweight and male. On *Lufthansa* flights, the candidates vary in age from 25 to 40 and are mainly the result of ground stress and aerophobia. A flight attendant from the airline also advised placing a cold Coke bottle behind the ear to prevent fainting.

The standard procedure on board is to wait for the passenger to faint before raising his legs to return the blood to the brain as quickly as possible.

These incidents can be also ascribed to vasovagal fainting. In such an instance, all the arteries dilate, draining blood from the head and, finally, the cranial nerve (the vagus) slows down the heart rate. It is a result of the failure to maintain an adequate venous return of the blood to the heart due to its pooling in the feet after prolonged standing or sitting (*see* **Blood Circulation**). This common cause of fainting, which is associated with symptoms of sweating, nausea and pallor, is also likely to happen through fear or anxiety and because of oxygen deficiency (*see* **Oxygen Deficiency**). It is a well-known phenomenon among aircrew.

The moment you feel dizzy, you need to get some volume in

fast. Any liquid intake (with the exception of alcohol) will do, whether cola, juice, plain mineral water, etc. There is also the other remedy of lowering your head between your knees to increase circulation if you are feeling hot or nauseated. In the case of elderly passengers, it may be prudent to eat lightly on board or to have a meal high in carbohydrates with coffee. There is evidence that drinking coffee at the end of such a meal prevents the drop in blood pressure.

The risk factors for the condition include dehydration, hypoxia (oxygen deficiency), changing position from seated to upright, prolonged sitting, alcohol, and medications for high blood pressure (such as beta-adrenergic blockers).

Douglas Adams, author of *The Hitchhiker's Guide to the Galaxy*, fainted during the dramatic cardiac injection scene in *Pulp Fiction* on a flight to Australia. An additional factor, such as strong emotion, can tip some individuals into syncope and consequently they should avoid watching violent films on aircraft.

EXERCISE

After a very long flight I always like to oxygenate by taking a really strenuous walk, expelling the toxins of recycled air and "petit fours."
ALAN CLARK, AUTHOR OF *DIARIES* AND
FORMER BRITISH MINISTER

Dynamic exercise is counterproductive on board aircraft because of the oxygen deficiency. Therefore a special "exercise-in-the-air" programme has been developed to deal with flying—which is after all a sedentary activity done in an environment that makes unusual demands on the body.

Airlines—both in the past (such as *SAS*), and currently (*British Airways*' "Well Being in the Air" and *Lufthansa*'s "Flyrobics" programs—the latter for flights of more than 10 hours)—have acknowledged the need for exercise during a flight and have provided their passengers with a suitable video on board.

Although the type and requirements of exercise vary with age, condition and occupation, for air travel there are two elements that need to be emphasized: to increase the intake of oxygen and to improve circulation. As there is a slight deficiency of oxygen on board because of cabin pressurization, passengers (particularly on long-haul flights) may benefit from exercises that improve their ability to absorb O_2. In fact, training can improve oxygen saturation levels by up to 20 percent.

PRE-FLIGHT EXERCISE

The best form of exercise to achieve a high-oxygen intake is one that makes use of the major muscle groups, such as jogging, running, squash, tennis, cycling and particularly swimming. Weight-training, because it does not develop the cardiovascular system, is unsuitable. To have any significant effect on oxygen saturation the exercise should be carried out three times a week for a period of 30 minutes. People in sedentary occupations should build up over a longer period, some six to eight weeks before a trip, than those who are active in their work.

The other type of exercise of interest to air travelers encourages circulation. Moderate dynamic exercise, such as brisk walking, not only decreases the tendency of the blood to clot but also exerts a protective influence on the circulatory system. Such an effect can last for several hours even after only 30 minutes of exercise.

IN-FLIGHT EXERCISE

On board, because of the limited space and lack of opportunity to walk, it is best to exercise in your seat. Moving your feet up and down to simulate walking can increase the blood flow rate significantly.

There are four further exercises that can be of help:

1. Contract the buttocks and abdominal muscles to stimulate circulation in the pelvis.
2. Stretch your arms and lift them up and down.
3. Open and clench your fists.
4. Rotate your ankle joints in large circles, extending them fully.

Keep fit in the air

✈ Caroline Rose Hunt, grande dame of Dallas society and daughter of the legendary H. L. Hunt, learned an important lesson about air travel when she flew on her first transatlantic trip to Paris in 1957. She lost her luggage and ever since has carried some essentials in her hand luggage.

At that time, as air travel was a great occasion, passengers got dressed up for a flight. "Nowadays, I try to travel in something comfortable," she says. "I have dispensed with the hat and gloves, but out of consideration for other passengers, I would not dream of wearing some of the attire such as sleeveless tanks and shorts I see others wearing. I do try to wear clothing which is not binding and is comfortable.

"I can't says much for the seats though, even in First Class. They are uncomfortable and I always put a pillow in the small of my back to compensate. I've complained to Bob Crandall of *American Airlines* about this problem but to no avail."

She believes in exercising in her seat and recommends three sorts of activity. The first is to open and clench your fists. The second is to tense all your muscles and then release them, while the third is to breathe deeply but erratically as this stimulates circulation.

When hot towels are handed around, she uses one for a dual purpose. She breathes in the hot air to open her nasal passages and then cleans her hands and face. A friend of hers actually takes along a small Thermos of boiling water and during the trip periodically breathes the steam to clear her nose and sinuses. She has noticed that the cabin ventilation exacerbates her allergies and she sneezes constantly. This is alleviated when she has taken antihistamine tablets.

FLYING CLOTHES

Sheepskin flying jackets and white scarves were once de rigueur *for air travel. Today*

> *it is casual, loose clothing (epitomized by the one-size sleepsuits issued by Air France on their First Class Sleeper Service) that sets the tone.*

Most passengers are aware that their ankles swell during a flight but are usually unaware that the same occurs to their stomachs (*see* **Gas Expansion**). As a result aircrew members tend to wear clothes which are either a size larger than they normally wear or have elasticated waistbands. The trend towards traveling in casual garments is in part helpful, but the items must not be too restrictive. Corsets, body-hugging jeans, panty girdles, tailored suits and constricting bras can lead to problems in-flight, such as chest pain or nausea on landing.

Restrictive clothing will cause the abdomen to press up against the diaphragm and sometimes even further towards the heart. The pain that is induced could be mistaken for angina. Another common complaint is air sickness experienced on descent or soon after landing. Such an incident can be attributed to the fact that the stomach contracts fairly rapidly in the higher pressure experienced during a descent, and the fact that the stomach walls contract even faster if the passenger is wearing tight clothing.

1. Footwear: Wear loose, comfortable shoes to allow for swollen ankles on board. Moccasins, sandals or "desert boots" are ideal. This is particularly relevant for older passengers as the swelling can last for several days post-flight.
2. Clothes: Avoid tight or restrictive undergarments or clothes on board as these can cause chest pain and

nausea before or after landing. The alternative is to change into a more comfortable outfit such as a track-suit, slippers or sockettes while in-flight.

GAS EXPANSION

Delta Air Lines, which carries 87 million people a year, has noticed an increase in the incidence of gas pain among its passengers.

The body contains a number of gas-filled cavities such as the ears, sinuses, lungs and stomach, which communicate with the surrounding atmosphere. In accordance with Boyle's Law, the gas will expand on ascent in an aircraft by some 30 to 35 percent, and while there is unrestricted access between the cavities and the surrounding atmosphere, this expansion will occur unnoticed. However, if this pressure build-up cannot be relieved it may cause considerable pain .

The most common site in the body for trapped gas is the middle ear, where a condition called *otitic baro-trauma* can arise. Here, inadequate ventilation causes pain in the middle ear, particularly if an infection is present. It can also result in temporary deafness, tinnitus or vertigo. The effects of pressure changes on the middle ear cavity is a good example of this. The cavity of the middle ear is separated from the outside by a thin diaphragm, the eardrum, which communicates with the back of the throat through the Eustachian tube, comprised of soft walls that collapse together.

During ascent, the expanding air easily escapes along the Eustachian tube and pressure is maintained equally on both sides of the ear drum. (The popping sensation sometimes experienced is due to the air escaping down this tube.)

During descent, the collapsed walls of the Eustachian tube tend to act as a valve preventing air from flowing back into the middle ear cavity. The resultant pressure build-up on the outside of the eardrum distorts the drum inward. As the degree of distortion increases with descent the pressure differential across the drum causes a sensation of fullness in the ear, a decrease in hearing and local pain. If the descent continues without equalization of pressure, the eardrum may perforate. In some passengers the rapid increase of pressure in the middle ear cavity can affect their organs of balance and cause vertigo.

When Leslie Lefkowitz of the Ritz-Carlton flew at the age of 16 for the first time, she experienced a sharp pain in an upper left tooth. What frightened her was that it came from nowhere. She begged for an aspirin from the flight atttendant to relieve her discomfort. Ever since she has always taken one on a flight in case that intolerable pain returned (*see* infected dental cavities, #3 below).

1. Pressure changes: Sometimes it is necessary to perform a maneuver to open the Eustachian tubes, such as yawning, swallowing or (in the case of babies) screaming. A more soothing alternative for the latter is to offer them a dummy or bottle. Should these actions fail to clear the ears, the *Valsalva manoeuvre* should be attempted. Here

you inhale and then close your nose with a thumb and forefinger and exhale—*keeping your mouth closed.*

2. Colds: In the case of inflammation of the middle ear or otitis media, it is advisable not to fly. For head colds (which may cause congestion and swelling of the lining of the Eustachian tube) or sinusitis (in which the lining of the sinus is swollen), a nasal decongestion spray may help to ease the pain. However, again it is better not to fly with such conditions. If you do fly and your hearing does not return to normal, you should seek medical advice urgently to prevent the risk of permanent damage to the middle ear. Parents often do not appreciate the damage that a child can suffer as a result of *otitis barotrauma.*

3. Infected cavities: As a general principle, any cavities or semi-cavities of the body that are either infected or inflamed are likely to cause pain and should be treated beforehand. These can include loose deep-seated dental fillings, intestinal infections and any areas where air circulates or has access, such as the thoracic cavity.

4. Surgery: Air enters the body during surgery and you should not travel until this air has been reabsorbed into the bloodstream. Otherwise, the gas may expand and cause a hemorrhage. Factors that delay healing include advanced age, steroid treatment, diabetes, obesity and smoking. Allow a reasonable period (at least a week) before considering air travel.

5. Plaster casts: Passengers with limbs in casts should consider having them split if they undertake long-haul flights. Air trapped within the cast can expand and compress the underlying tissue, causing a circulatory obstruction.

6. Stomach: A common semi-cavity that is usually over-looked is the stomach, where gas can expand by about 30 percent during a flight. For this reason, car-bonated drinks and foods such as peas, beans, roughage, cabbage and cauliflower should be avoided. (*Also see* **Flying Clothes** and **Properties of Air**).

HEARING

Temporary hearing loss is an unusual consequence of flying, as some passengers may be vulnerable to noise (such as that of the jet engines) on board an aircraft.

Prolonged moderate-to-high noise levels are well known for producing a phenomenon called Temporary Threshold Shift (TTS). This consists of a decrease in auditory sensitivity which can last from minutes to days or even weeks depending on the nature of the noise and the length of time a person is exposed to it. The stimuli that have been known to induce hearing loss have usu-ally consisted of very high intensity, spectrally simple signals such as pure tones or broad band noise over rel-atively short periods of time (up to a few hours). The condition can be debilitating, particularly if a passenger has to attend a meeting or other important engagement soon after arrival.

If your hearing is sensitive it is best to wear earplugs on board and to ensure that your seat is well forward of the engines, where the noise levels are lower. Some airlines, such as *JAL*, supply Sony earphones which neutralize background noise.

HUMIDITY

A component of cabin air that is usually overlooked is the moisture content, as few passengers realize that it helps prevent infection.

The humidity level within the cabin tends to be low, partly because the outside air at high altitude contains 66 percent less water than at sea level (about 0.15 g/kg of dry air compared to 10 g/kg respectively) and partly due to the fact that the air, which enters at a temperature of about 54°C/65°F below zero, has to be heated.

The relative humidity in aircraft, which can vary from 2 to 23 percent, is far from the comfort zone of between 30 and 65 percent recommended by both the Association of Heating, Refrigeration and Air-Conditioning Engineers (ASHRAE) and the National Institute of Occupational Safety and Health (NIOSH) (*see* **Cabin Air Quality**). Low levels of humidity, together with contributing factors such as tiredness, stress, age (the elderly, children and babies seem to suffer most) and antibody status increase our susceptibility to infection.

Low humidity causes the filtering functions of the nose and upper airways to be compromised. When air is breathed in, it enters the nose, passes down the trachea and through the upper airways to the lungs. On its way to the lungs the air is heated, humidified and filtered. The important factor in this process is found in the cellular structure of the lining of upper airways. Along this route from the trachea to the bronchi and the bronchioles lies the body's protection network against infection. The surface of these cells is covered in fine hair-like projections called *cilia*.

There is a layer of mucus around the cilia which is continually secreted by goblet cells. The cilia beat constantly, much like corn moving in a cornfield, and carry the layer of mucus up towards the back of the throat where it is swallowed. Any inhaled microorganisms or specks of dust which have escaped the hairs in the nose soon get trapped in this layer of mucus and are returned to the back of the throat, where they are swallowed.

In environments with low humidity, such as aircraft, inhaled air reduces the moisture content from the mucus to such an extent that the layer becomes viscous and concentrated. When this occurs it is more difficult for the cilia to beat and the mucus, rather than being moved along to the back of the throat, remains in the respiratory tract for a longer period, where it can cause infection.

Of the microorganisms carried by the air, it is viruses—particularly respiratory viruses—which survive better than bacteria in low humidity. This could explain the fact that passengers tend to suffer from upper respiratory infections post-flight. The other reason, of course, is inadequate cabin air filtration.

There are several examples of airborne viruses that cause disease. Influenza, which infects the upper and lower respiratory tracts, can in its mild form cause flu, but in susceptible people this can progress to viral pneumonia. In the case of the common cold, many different viruses can be responsible.

1. The obvious method of preventing infection on board an aircraft through low humidity is to drink water (see **Thirst**).
2. Fly on crowded flights. Moisture from other passengers' breathing and perspiration can increase the relative humidity dramatically. In the instance of an eight-hour flight in a DC-10 with 265 passengers, the humidity level can rise to 20 percent; the same flight with only 108 passengers sees this level fall to 2 percent. Aircraft which have recirculated air have a higher humidity level than those with only a 100-percent fresh airflow.
3. Frequent flyers should regularly use rehydration gels or moisturizers, such as Prescriptives Flight Age Cream, to protect their skin from the drying, aging effects of low humidity levels.

HYPERVENTILATION

Hyperventilation, which is common among passengers, has an unusual feature (known to those who participate in certain voodoo ceremonies, particularly mutilation): it anaesthetizes the participant.

This condition, which denotes fast or over-breathing, affects a large proportion of pilots during training, as well as experienced flight crew on the occasions when they are under mental stress. The pattern among air travelers is similar, and it is the most inexperienced flyers who tend to breathe too fast.

The most obvious trigger on board is the oxygen deficiency, or hypoxia, that causes increased ventilation, among other things, as the body makes an effort to compensate for the lack of O_2 (*see* **Oxygen Deficiency**). Another trigger which is commonplace on the ground (where the condition is usually described as hysterical panting) is mental and emotional disturbance. However, during a flight there are sufficient environmental influences such as motion sickness, body vibration, air turbulence and a hot, stuffy cabin, as well as the possible contributory factors such as anxiety and emotional stress. To a lesser degree, there are certain drugs that can stimulate breathlessness such as stimulants and oral contraceptives.

The symptoms of the condition are dizziness, palpitations, a tingling sensation in the limbs or face and pain, discomfort or a tightness in the chest. The last symptom can lead to hyperventilation being mistaken for an attack of angina.

When hyperventilation occurs, large amounts of carbon dioxide are exhaled. Low levels of CO_2 in the blood upsets the acid-alkali balance and the blood becomes more àlkaline, leading to alkalosis (*see* **Mountain Sickness**). Essentially, the condition inhibits the catalytic activity of enzymes, which can affect the cardiovascular and central nervous systems. The hyperventilator can experience severe chest pain and signs such as blurred vision and dizziness as the blood flow to the brain decreases with the onset of hypoxia (oxygen deficiency).

As a group, hyperventilation affects men and women equally; those who are most prone are meticulous, hardworking perfectionists.

1. If you find yourself overbreathing, rebreathe the air you have exhaled by breathing into a paper bag. Also, make a conscious effort to breathe more slowly.
2. As hyperventilation can chalk up losses of moisture, it would be prudent to drink lots of water to rehydrate your body after an episode.
3. Some air travelers who often overbreathe on aircraft may find that they are breathing incorrectly. Instead of taking deep breaths they are indulging in shallow, fast breaths. An easy way to check for this at home is to relax either in an armchair or on the floor with one hand on your chest and the other on your abdomen. When you breathe normally your chest rather than your abdomen should rise. Incorrect breathing can be corrected by consulting a respiratory physiotherapist.
4. On the other hand, passengers whose chronic hyperventilation is associated with anxiety disorders may need sedation before the flight. Check with your doctor or physician.

The so-called antidotes which should be avoided are alcohol and supplemental oxygen, which may sometimes be offered by a flight attendant. Both can aggravate rather than alleviate hyperventilation.

JETLAG

*When a lot of different remedies are proposed for a
disease, that means the disease cannot be cured.*
ANTON CHEKHOV, DRAMATIST AND
QUALIFIED DOCTOR

Jetlag is one of the most common words associated
with aviation. Most passengers experience it after trips
of over three hours either west or east.

The main cause of jetlag is the disruption of the
body's circadian rhythms, more commonly known as
our 24-hour clock. These rhythms were discovered by
Professor Franz Halberg in the early 1960s when he
placed seven women in a dark cave for two weeks and
observed that their physiological cycle (or biological
clock) was actually 24 hours and 24 minutes long. In
total darkness, therefore, the circadian rhythm "free-
runs" and averages between 24.5 and 25.5 hours.

These internal rhythms or cycles are associated
with hormone secretions from various glands including the master gland, the pituitary. The hormones regu-
late about 100 different activities such as arousing
people from sleep, causing body temperature variations and decreasing mental alertness and manual dex-
terity after midnight. In addition, there are external
synchronizers such as natural light, darkness and food
intake that contribute to the complex workings of the
body clock.

When this mechanism is disturbed, as by a flight
crossing a number of time zones, several days are
required to reset it. As a rule of thumb, a recovery rate
of one day per hour lost or gained as you travel across

time zones is required. In the case of a transatlantic trip, for example, it takes about five days to readjust.

Jetlag affects people in different ways and to varying degrees, and can depend on factors such as their chronological and physiological age, their sensitivity to environmental synchronizers and their self-selected patterns of exposure to social and sunlight "cues" in each time zone. In some exceptional cases, jetlag is almost non-existent (see "Jetlag-free," page 80). It is believed that psychological factors also play their part.

Common symptoms of jetlag are extreme fatigue resulting in diminished mental and physical performance, insomnia, stomach upsets (such as constipation), aches and pains, irritability and disorientation. Such symptoms are more prominent on west–east flights where the day is shortened. This has given rise to the adage "flying west is best," a phenomenon that conforms to Professor Halberg's observations about the body's tendency towards a longer rather than a shorter day.

The fact remains that once the circadian rhythms are disturbed, they are difficult to readjust. This is not surprising as the earth, a body which has a mass of 6,600 trillion tons, is responsible for their origin through its rotation every 24 hours. Such an understanding is of little consolation to the hundreds of thousands of pilots who are tripped up on each flight by jetlag. One of them, Captain David Fleming who has been flying for 26 years with *British Airways*, speaks on their behalf: "Circadian rhythms must be one of the strongest forces in the body."

Sir Martin Jacomb, chairman of the British Council and the Prudential Corporation, has found an ideal answer to the problem. "When I didn't deny the existence of jetlag, it encouraged my body to minimize the effects," he said. "The body does know what is happening and like a sensitive computer it can adjust accordingly to synchronize the differences in time zones."

This attitude runs counter to the macho display of many business flyers who dismiss the fact that their bodies are affected by dysrhythmia. They force themselves to come into the office after a gruelling flight and do little work while they are there.

Solutions for jetlag abound from the simple to the expensive, and as individuals respond slightly differently to the disruption in their circadian rhythms, you should choose a method that is most suitable to your needs. Success depends on the degree to which the effects of the cabin environment are taken into account. They are part of the overall strategy of arriving in better shape.

The best methods include the use of synchronizers to reset your body clock. Sleep, daylight and social cues are strong synchronizers that produce significant results.

SLEEP

Sleep is undoubtedly the top countermeasure to jetlag and flight fatigue for passengers and flightcrews worldwide. On long-haul flights, sleep for part of the trip. If this is not possible there are "napping strategies" you can try. A single 70- to 120-minute nap taken prior to the flight can reduce the decline in performance over the subsequent 24-hour period. This is an excellent device for those who need to be active when they arrive at their destination. The only adverse effect of such strategic napping is the grogginess that lasts for about 15 minutes after awakening. A shorter nap, which produces a less dazed sensation, can also be taken between appointments or activities once you land at your destination. To derive maximum benefit, take this short nap after lunch, between 2 and 3 P.M. Make sure you avoid caffeine for some three hours beforehand. Captain Tim Ward of *Air New Zealand* finds a 45-minute nap at this time of day an ideal way of gaining "sleep credits."

Another strategy is to stay up to as near midnight as you can at your destination before going to bed. Such an approach fits in with the body's natural free-running rhythms, which are longer than 24 hours. It should be repeated over two or three successive nights.

DAYLIGHT

Bright light, particularly sunlight, is another important synchronizer. Time spent outdoors at your destination is an excellent way to get your internal body clock to coincide with local time.

Exposure to bright artificial light, which has an intensity of early morning daylight, can also influence the circadian pacemaker. Bright glare-free light levels of about 1,000 lux (equivalent to two 150-watt light bulbs placed 3 feet away) can increase performance; doubling that amount to 2,000 lux can help change the setting of your biological clock. Air travelers who cannot spend time outdoors should arrange to increase the light levels indoors to benefit from this synchronizer. The Okura Hotel in Tokyo is one place where guests are provided with 2,500 lux light boxes as part of the hotel's "beat jetlag" regime.

SOCIAL CUES

Group travel has been found to be better than individual travel for helping people make the adjustment to changes in time zones. Social psychologists have shown that there is increased motivation when performance tests are taken in groups rather than in individual isolation. As solitary travelers tend to take longer to adjust, it is preferable, should you have important negotiations to make at your destination, to undertake these with the help of associates.

The discovery of this synchronizer arose from the Pavlovian response of dogs, who were found to adjust better to changes in their sleep patterns in the presence of other dogs. Aircrew from *Aeroflot* later used this method to their advantage when they slept at Soviet embassies around the world but kept to Moscow time.

The Four Seasons Hotel in New York offers its guests a unique service according to Thomas Gurtner, the general manager, as it operates 24 hours a day. This enables the guests to sleep, eat or clean their clothes anytime they desire. As the hotel was designed by I. M. Pei, it provides air passengers who have been closeted in a cramped space the additional bonus of the largest standard rooms in the city.

PSYCHOLOGICAL ELEMENT

The most neglected synchronizer is the psychological, which is used effectively by the U.S. Army. Their successful antidote to jetlag is to issue an order for all troops who travel by air, either on combat missions or on training exercises, to set their watches to the local time of their destination and to act accordingly. If it is time to eat, they eat; if it is night, they go to sleep.

The proliferation of pet cures—such as earthing the feet in brown paper bags—and numerous products for jetlag is also due to the high placebo effect of such psychologically soothing remedies. They work for some passengers.

THE ULTIMATE $8,400 CURE

A unique although limited solution to jetlag is provided on a single air route, the North Atlantic. There is near-perfect integration of circadian rhythms when you fly *Concorde* west. The five time zones that separate Europe from North America shrink to almost zero on a London or Paris *Concorde* flight to New York. Both *British Airways* and *Air France* offer passengers the opportunity of returning the same day, with a 3-hour work period in the city. Such a method is favoured by the financial and business community. Robert Scott, a banker with Morgan Stanley, says "Jetlag is not a problem when I fly *Concorde*, especially going west." You can save $1,500 if you fly to London via Paris with *Air France Concorde*.

THE JETLAG PILL

Melatonin is a hormone produced by the body that helps to synchronize the body clock. Although is has not yet been approved by the U.S. Food and Drug Administration, synthetic melatonin is on sale in the U.S. at health food stores as a nutritional supplement. It would be prudent to treat the hormone with caution until the FDA grants a licence for its use as a remedy for jetlag.

Jetlag-free

✈ Dan Snively from Los Angeles has a quality that would be much admired and envied by other frequent flyers. He does not succumb to jetlag.

A businessman in his fifties, he attributes this characteristic to the power of positive thinking.

"Air travel," he says, "is a waste of time. It does not exist. The minute I leave my mind is elsewhere. It could already be at the destination where I would go over the presentation I've got to do." There is one device that has helped him with his mental attitude: he keeps his watch on L.A. time even after he arrives. He does not mind calculating the time difference during his stay at his destination.

He also has difficulty sleeping on board, and after a night flight on *Delta Air Lines* is rather tired. As is to be expected he is dismissive of this sleep loss. "It is mind over matter," he observes. "I'll make it up tonight in the hotel. But I'll stay up late. It's a matter of survival."

He does not follow any of the advice given in this book about how much he eats, drinks, sleeps or exercises on board. He strongly affirms that he is too busy running his own company to worry about air travel. For him, jetlag is a luxury he cannot afford.

MEALS

Although airborne meals are often criticized, few people realize that it is not the ingredients that are at fault but those who consume them. Their sense of taste is distorted by the flight environment.

Though there are few technical restrictions on the sort of food that can be served at high altitude, the cabin and the atmosphere impose their own limitations. Space is at a premium and the kitchen is usually pared down to a single piece of equipment (a convection oven, as microwaves interfere with the communications systems).

In general, food is prepared on the ground, pre-cooked or partially cooked before the flight and reheated several hours later in the aircraft's galley. This process is a challenge for the great chefs who have provided impeccable cuisines for airlines in the past. No expense is spared in these creations and the highest quality ingredients are used. Anton Edelmann, *maître chef des cuisines* at the Savoy and on occasions responsible for menus on *British Airways*, says, "We have to select dishes which won't object to being reheated so we can't use puff pastry, which can split during regeneration, or certain sauces."

Another aspect that the chefs have to contend with is the dehydrating atmosphere in the cabin—and the solution is not found in the provision of rehydratable meals and water guns for the passengers! Sauces are the obvious answer and tend to proliferate on menus in the Premium Classes. Passengers also undergo a physiological change which chefs have to take into account. Raymond Blanc, who runs Le Manoir aux Quat' Saisons and supervises the catering operation of *Virgin Atlantic*, observes, "A dish you try on the ground will taste totally different at high altitude." Chefs have found that the sensation of taste is not as reliable during air travel as it is on the ground. This is due in part to the fact that the finer distinctions of taste depend on the sense of smell, which is blunted by the cabin environment. Paul Betts of the *Financial Times* suggests, as a rule of thumb, only eating food that looks appetizing.

Kurt Hafner, the chief of catering at *British Airways*, explains that as a result sauces and dressings need to have a strong flavor. He recommends that salad dressings contain sharper ingredients, such as chili and ginger, while sauces should include ingredients like herbs and mustard. Raymond Blanc finds that dishes such as coq au vin and *boeuf bourgignon* are successful because they are moist and have good strong flavors. Caviar, with its distinctive sharpness, is much prized by some passengers and is on the menu of three airlines, *United* (which has beluga), *Lufthansa* (sevruga and keta) and *Delta* (sevruga).

The same taste principle applies to wines where vintages with savoury and penetrating flavours predominate over the more subtle. "The New World wines, like Nobilo from New Zealand, show character in the air as on the ground," says Peter Nixson, manager of wine and beverages, *British Airways*. "The nuances of a Chablis or Claret don't stand up to the rigours of dehydration which impairs our sense of smell."

The acidity in a wine or champagne and its tannic property tend to be accented on board. In spite of this, champagne is still the most popular drink in the skies, according to Peter Nixson. However, *British Airways* has taken steps to rectify this acidic problem by becoming the first airline to introduce a unique champagne blended to taste better at high altitudes. "The Piper-Heidsieck champagne," says Peter Nixson, "is rounder and fuller in the mouth and has lost that aggressive edge."

Children's palates are also catered for by airlines such as *Delta*, who provide Funfeast meals that ensure their appetites are stimulated. Snacks feature peanut butter sandwiches, while lunch and dinner can consist of items such as pepperoni pizza and gummy candy (these must be requested at least six hours prior to departure).

Cathay Pacific offers a bonanza of special meals, serving over 31 varieties, all of which have to be ordered 24 hours before departure. These include vegetarian (ovo-lacto, vegan, Oriental or Indian), religious (Kosher, Muslim or Hindu nonvegetarian), medical (diabetic, gluten-free, liquid or high-fiber), diet (low sodium, low cholesterol, low fat or protein), and baby foods. *Air Canada* provides a nutricuisine for its Business Class and as a second meal choice in Economy that is not only low in salts, sugar and fat but also high in complex carbohydrates.

When you touch down, or before you take off, some hotels offer you healthy menus that follow the American Heart Association's dietary guidelines for total fat, saturated fatty acids, cholesterol and sodium. The Ritz-Carlton hotels serve Cuisine Vitale, in which 241 recipes have been approved by the AHA.

FOOD IN SPACE

The process of preparing, serving and eating meals has been found, during the last three decades, to play a powerful role in boosting the morale of astronauts and cosmonauts. The liquid mixtures of amino acids, sugar and vitamins that placed little demand on their intestines were a failure partly due to their "instantness," lack of texture and to their foul taste!

Early space voyagers on the Vostok, Voskhod and Mercury missions consumed unappetizing dried food bars, either vacuum-packed or freeze-dried, and purées and juices out of squeezable aluminium tubes. The purées, which consisted of meat, vegetables, cereals, processed cheese and prunes, were squeezed into the mouth through a short polystyrene straw.

Over time, rehydrated forms of food were introduced to make meals more palatable. Fresh fruit and vegetables became part of the cargo carried to Salyut space stations and appeared on the menu of the Shuttle and Skylab. The Americans also offered what was termed natural form (NF) items such as peanuts, bread, pecan cookies and beef jerky, and thermostabilized (heated) foods.

On the Shuttle, each meal is labelled according to a six-day master menu and the various contents can be rearranged or supplemented by different items from the pantry. At mealtimes it can take up to an hour to prepare food for the seven astronauts on board. Servings are placed in trays with special compartments, each food package held in place in friction-fit recesses while the cutlery is restrained by magnets. Velcro strips line the underside of the tray to enable it to be attached either to the astronaut's lap or to the table top for dining.

(For a look at a typical menu on board the Space Shuttle, *see* Table 7 in Appendix A.)

MEDICAL KITS

Although medical incidents on board air-craft are uncommon, medical kits have proved to be effective in the majority of

> *such cases. "By virtue of having a well-*
> *equipped medical kit," says Dr. Eric*
> *Peters of SAS's Medical Department, "the*
> *airlines save several costly diversions*
> *every year."*

Civil aviation regulations require all airlines to carry some form of medical kit which contains supplies for first-aid and a doctor's use, and portable oxygen canisters to deal with problems that may arise in-flight.

The kit is usually tailored to meet a wide range of needs from airsickness, stomach upsets, cuts, headaches and toothaches to the rare medical emergency, such as a heart attack. Annette Bauder of *Lufthansa*, who trained as a nurse, attended to a passenger who collapsed from cardiac failure on a short flight of 40 minutes. "I recognized the symptom of angina pectoris," she says, "and when I took his blood pressure I found it was high." She gave him a nitrolingual tablet and saved his life. He was in his fifties, overweight, a nonsmoker but had had too much alcohol and too little sleep. In the *British Airways* "M5 medical case," the contents are typical of major European carriers and include a stethoscope, a blood-pressure cuff (sphygmomanometer), obstetric delivery pack and a syringe and needles. There is also a comprehensive selection of 27 drugs, from the revolutionary sublingual spray that acts on the symptoms of angina in 30 seconds, to others that treat pain, anxiety, diarrhea, diabetes, hypoglycemia, asthmatic attacks, nausea, bleeding, allergic reactions, and cardiac and respiratory conditions. In addition, *British Airways* has two further kits, "M1" (for short-haul flights) and "M2" (for long-haul). The first contains nasal decongestants, simple painkillers, throat lozenges, etc., while the second includes anti-malarial tablets, water-testing equipment and insect repellent.

The basis of the contents of medical boxes on aircraft can vary according to regulations, the availability of space, weight restrictions, and the observed need for such equipment. *Lufthansa, SAA, Qantas* and *Air New Zealand* exceed the International Air Transport Association standards for medical kits. The Federal Aviation Authority, for example, specifies for U.S. airlines only the minimum contents a kit should contain to be able to treat problems such as asthma attacks, allergic reactions, anginal episodes and hypoglycemia (*see* Table 8 in Appendix A). *American Airlines*, in addition, has a medical physician on call 24 hours a day, seven days a week. Should the need arise for cabin crew or passengers on board, this doctor could be reached at any time by radio.

Dr. Sandy Dawson of *Air New Zealand*, which has a high proportion of long-haul passengers, describes the contents of their medical kit as having a pyramidal structure. At the base there are items for daily use, such as a stethoscope and nebulizer mask for asthma, while at the top, a high-tech semi-automatic defibrillator for use in cardiopulmonary resuscitation (CPR). *Qantas* was one of the first airlines to introduce the semi-automatic version of this piece of equipment, which can be operated by cabin crew. This development was pioneered by Dr. Eric Donaldson and prevented many stressful en route diversions. The passengers who benefit are those suffering sudden cardiac problems. "There are a few people walking around today," says Dr. Donaldson, "who would not be without the use of the defibrillator." *Virgin* is the only other airline that carries it.

In a survey carried out in 1989 on the efficacy of the U.S. medical kit over a period of a year, the usage frequency was found to be once in every 1900 flights, or for one in every 150,000 air travelers. The investigation, conducted on *United Airlines*, found that the most commonly used medical supplies were the stethoscope, blood-pressure cuff (needed in 80 percent of the incidents) and (in 60 percent of cases) supplemental oxygen (*see* **Supplemental Oxygen**).

The kit proved to be useful in over 80 percent of the in-flight emergencies that could be categorized into one of seven major diagnostic groupings. These included fainting/near fainting (29 percent), heart/chest pain (16 percent), asthma/lung disease/shortness of breath (10 percent), allergic reactions (5 percent), seizures (4 percent), anxiety (4 percent) and diabetes (3 percent). Illness appeared to be random and not associated with any aircraft type or flight duration. (For a list of common in-flight illnesses *see* Table 9 in Appendix A.)

Although medical kits require the permission of the captain to be used, because they contain restricted drugs, the chance of a doctor being on board is usually high. In a survey, in 81 percent of cases there was a physician on board, while in the remaining cases there was a nurse or paramedic on board.

MEDICATIONS

The effects and side-effects of drugs can be heightened in the confines of the pressurized cabin. This is due to the interaction

*between the physiological stresses of flight,
particularly oxygen lack, and medicines.
As the former alters brain function, the
actions of any drugs that affect the brain
will be altered, too. Medicines and drugs
that fall into such a category include antihistamines, acetazolamide, fat-soluble
beta-blockers, alcohol and psychotropes.*

Almost all the antihistamines produce side-effects such
as drowsiness, vomiting, diarrhea, fatigue, dry mouth
and tinnitus, and are commonly prescribed for "cold
cures," motion sickness, hay-fever and urticaria (nettle
rash). Perhaps the gastrointestinal symptoms are mistaken by passengers for food poisoning.

Acetazolamide is used to treat glaucoma and to regu-
larize breathing at altitude (*see* **Mountain Sickness**).
Among the psychotrope group are hypnotics and seda-
tives, tranquillizers and antidepressants, marijuana, LSD
and opium. Therefore, if the passenger is under medication or plans to use over-the-counter medicines on
board he or she should consult a physician beforehand.
His or her doctor may want to decrease the patient's
dosage for the duration of the flight, because of the
cabin environment's effect on medications, that is, to
increase their potency.

The interaction between oxygen lack and drugs can
also have other effects on the brain. For example, there
have been cases of memory loss when the hypnotic tria-
zolam (0.5 gm) was taken on board to encourage sleep
and minimize jetlag. This benzodiazepine, which has a
short half-life of 2.6 hours, caused transient global
amnesia that lasted for several hours after landing. In

each case, a moderate amount of alcohol, such as a glass of wine, was consumed. Consequently, the National Westminster Bank have excluded sleeping tablets from their travel kit. "The other reason," says Dr. David Murray Bruce, "is that under the influence of a hypnotic you won't be alert enough in an emergency."

Such episodes suggest that it is best to exercise caution when using this medication to avoid jetlag (*see* **Jetlag**), particularly if alcohol is imbibed during the flight. A more common experience with tranquillizers taken for aerophobia on board is severe depression, which cannot be shaken no matter how idyllic the passenger's destination.

There are a couple of other examples that illustrate the unusual relationship between drug dosage and the flight environment. Diabetic passengers should increase their dose of insulin when flying west and decrease it when they are eastward bound on long-haul, to bring their insulin levels into line with the time zone they are flying to. Another factor that they should take into account is that the consumption of excessive alcohol can precipitate hypoglycemia (*see* **Diabetes**).

On the other hand, epileptic passengers may well have to increase their dosage because oxygen lack, over-breathing, fatigue and stress can provoke seizure. In fact, those whose condition is poorly controlled should be advised to increase their medication 24 hours before take-off and maintain a high dose until they arrive at their final destination. Thereafter, there should be a gradual reduction of the dosage. Certain drug groups, such as salicylates, female sex hormones, catecholamines and analeptics have been found to cause hyperventilation (*see* **Hyperventilation**).

A final reminder for all passengers on medication is to consult with their doctor and to take it regularly during the flight based on home time, and to adjust the regimen only after they arrive in the new time zone.

MOUNTAIN SICKNESS

The connection between mountain sickness and air travel may not be apparent and may even seem odd, but the former can inadvertently be provoked by the latter.

The first link arises from the fact that there is an analogy between flying and mountaineering. Both activities occur at altitude. As modern aircraft are pressurized to altitudes of between 5,000 and 8,000 feet, passengers can be whisked to the height of a minor peak in the Alps without moving a limb.

However, there is a corresponding increase in blood pressure, heart rate and respiration. This physiological effort can account for the inexplicable fatigue some passengers feel, even after short flights. Additional factors, such as the amount of alcohol consumed or food eaten, or stress experienced at the airport, can also be contributory factors.

Mountain sickness, or acute mountain sickness (AMS) as the benign syndrome is known, is characterized by nausea, headache, loss of appetite, dizziness and sleep disturbance. The condition is quite harmless but the symptoms should not be ignored in case it develops into a more serious form characterized by cerebral or pulmonary oedema (water on the brain or lungs).

It seems to be caused by the alkalinity of the blood and the presence of nitrogen bubbles (*see* **Decompression Sickness**). As our bodies adapt to compensate for the low oxygen pressure at altitude, we breathe more quickly and therefore expel more carbon dioxide. One of the functions of carbon dioxide is that it keeps the blood acidic, and so the loss of this gas can cause the blood to be more alkaline. There is also a release of nitrogen bubbles on ascent, and some experts believe that these small bubbles are responsible for increased blood-clotting and certain other complications of mountain sickness. The small and large blood clots often found in the blood vessels of high-altitude victims may be the result of nitrogen bubbles and may affect the blood vessels' permeability.

But people do not have to ascend to a great height to be affected by AMS, as it can equally occur at levels of 8,000 feet or below. A 1989 survey of 400 people at U.S. ski resorts located at 6,600 feet demonstrated that the condition affected 25 percent of skiers. The illness was short-lived, however, and the symptoms disappeared within the first 72 hours.

Factors such as age or physical fitness are no guarantee against the condition. Studies on several thousands of visitors who come to the resorts in the Colorado Rockies have shown that men are more vulnerable than women because they tend to be more active, while children (rather than adolescents) and adults are more susceptible to the malignant form of the illness than are the elderly, unless the latter have a condition that predisposes them to it (such as cardiac or pulmonary complications). This may in part be due to the fact that the elderly tend to climb more slowly. The rate of ascent is a crucial factor in preventing mountain sickness.

Passengers who fly direct on long-haul routes to mountain resorts and go at once into the mountains may be at greater risk than those arriving more slowly by ground transportation. They are likely already to be slightly hypoxic (oxygen-deficient) and exhibiting symptoms such as headache, fatigue, mental sluggishness and perhaps oedema (water retention in tissues) and breathing difficulties. Some evidence suggests that when established circadian rhythms are altered by crossing several time zones, susceptibility to hypoxia (oxygen deficiency) is increased, perhaps not only during a long-haul flight but for several days after arrival as well.

The answer is to let your body acclimatize, because the kidneys can adjust over a few days to the increased alkalinity and allow the body to adapt to the lack of oxygen. For those who cannot or will not take time to acclimatize, acetazolamide (diamox) offers protection against AMS. This drug increases arterial oxygenation during sleep and consequently decreases mountain sickness symptoms in the morning. Another method is to use the Gamow or pressure bag (see Appendix B), which will increase oxygen pressure in the lungs within one minute.

THE OCEAN OF AIR

At 150 miles above the earth, the astronaut John Glenn made an interesting observation when he orbited the planet. "One of the things that surprised me about

> *the flight was the percentage of the earth covered by clouds," he said. "The clouds were nearly solid over central Africa and extended over most of the Indian Ocean. Western Australia was clear but it was cloudy again from eastern Australia almost all the way across the Pacific... There were large storms north of my course, and though I was nearly three quarters of a million feet above the clouds, I could clearly see lightning in them."*

Few people realize that the thin mantle of air, the atmosphere around the earth which sustains life, also provides a medium for aircraft to fly through. You may like, therefore, to understand this movement of air in the sky.

A pilot has to navigate the aircraft through this ocean of air just as a sea captain guides his ship over the water. "Sailing is not too far removed from flying," says Captain Jock Lowe, of the *Concorde* fleet at *British Airways*. Before each flight pilots have to check in at a briefing room to obtain a weather chart of their proposed air route. Based on this and the traffic at the other end, they will calculate the quantity of fuel to be carried on board.

Clouds are essential to pilots as they are important visible clues to what is going on in the sky. These condensed droplets of water, which can produce rain, snow or hail and the invisible winds, are part of air masses that comprise the weather.

There are five basic words to describe different types of clouds:

1. stratus (layer clouds)
2. nimbus (rain clouds)
3. alto (high clouds)
4. cumulus (piled high, accumulated clouds)
5. cirrus (feathery, curled and ice-crystal clouds).

A combination such as cumulo-nimbus clouds resemble pictures of castles and mountains and tower majestically in the sky. Small cumulus can develop into thunderstorms that move as high as 80,000 feet. Such a feature of severe weather is something that pilots are most careful to circumvent by a distance of at least 20 miles. Weather radar, which can detect droplets of moisture, is useful in helping pilots pinpoint these clouds, particularly at night.

Air masses can be stable when they tend to stay in balance, falling towards the earth at a steady rate, and unstable when they are inclined to rise. There is the example of a cold air mass passing over warm land. The heat from the land warms the lower levels of the air mass and creates convective currents. As the warm air rises, the cold air falls. This upward and downward movement causes turbulence. When it occurs in skies without clouds this phenomenon is known as clear-air turbulence (CAT).

Winds on air routes can also speed up or slow down an aircraft. Headwinds can slow down an aircraft as they blow directly against the set course. (The exception to this is *Concorde*, which travels at such a great speed that even a 50-mph headwind has little effect.) In contrast, a tailwind that blows in the same direction as the aircraft is flying increases its speed, as does a jet stream. This narrow band of high-altitude winds, located at about 36,000 feet, moves eastward providing a great boost with its high velocity. Pilots flying east to west on the North Atlantic route try to avoid the jet stream, but on the return journey out of the U.S. they make an effort to find it as this can cut flying time by at least an hour.

OXYGEN DEFICIENCY

Oxygen lack has fascinated many scientists over the years. Joseph Barcroft from Cambridge was so curious that he lived for six days in a glass box where the oxygen supply was gradually depleted until on the last day it was down to 10 percent of the atmosphere — the equivalent of being at an altitude of 19,000 feet. It was termed a heroic experiment and he felt quite ill at the end.

Although the proportion of gases such as oxygen, nitrogen and carbon dioxide remains the same in the atmosphere no matter the altitude, as you go higher the partial pressure of each decreases (*see* **Properties of Air** and Table 10 in Appendix A). Oxygen deficiency, which is technically known as *hypoxia*, occurs when there is a decrease in the partial pressure of inspired oxygen (PIO_2), such as happens in an aircraft or on a mountaintop. The PIO_2 at sea level is 150 mmHg; at altitude it can fall to 60 mmHg, decreasing the oxygen level in the blood to 89 percent or below.

Most passengers at rest in an aircraft with cabin altitudes between 5,000 and 8,000 feet will experience little discomfort, with blood oxygen levels of 95 to 93 percent. Such a small degree of oxygen deficiency is termed mild hypoxia.

But at levels of 89 percent or less (equivalent to altitudes of about 10,000 feet and above), the effects of hypoxia become more apparent. Of all the tissue cells, the brain cells are the most sensitive to lack of oxygen. The areas of the brain most affected at low cabin altitudes are those associated with the powers of judgement, self-criticism and accurate performance.

Hypoxia in passengers is usually a short-term condition. As soon as they are back on the ground and a normal oxygen supply is restored, it disappears.

There are some individuals who may have lower blood oxygen saturation levels than average because of either their health or personal habits. Passengers with cardiovascular and respiratory disease, blood disorders or neurological conditions would fit into this category. They should consult their physician or the medical department of the airline before flying.

Other passengers who are likely to experience some discomfort are smokers, drinkers (particularly those who regularly drink large amounts of alcohol), the overweight, and those on medication for a cold or allergy.

Smokers can decrease their blood oxygen levels by between 4 and 8 percent before they even take off. The reason is that carbon monoxide, the chief component in tobacco smoke, has 300 times greater affinity for hemoglobin than oxygen, and therefore will displace it readily to form carboxyhemoglobin (see **Cabin Air Quality**). The effects of alcohol and other drugs, such as antihistamines, also contribute to oxygen deficiency (see **Medications**). Obesity causes a person to be more sensitive to low blood oxygen levels because a greater volume of tissue has to be supplied with blood than is true of people at a more desirable weight.

There is a natural method of alleviating oxygen deficiency (see **The Wonder Juice**).

OZONE

Ozone (O_3), which provides vital protection against the sun's ultra-violet radiation, is also a cabin air pollutant.

Ozone gas is found in the stratosphere, where it forms a broad layer around the earth at altitudes of between 40,000 and 180,000 feet. Within this ozonosphere the maximum concentration can rise to nearly 10 parts per million by volume (ppmv) at 100,000 feet, but decreases to less than 1 ppmv at higher or lower levels. There are also variations according to latitude, season, time of day and weather conditions. In the northern hemisphere the ozone concentration is highest in spring and, at latitudes above 40 degrees north, exists mainly in low-pressure areas.

The gas was first encountered in aviation when there were complaints about the corrosion of the natural rubber drop-down oxygen masks in the Comet and the Boeing 707. When this was investigated in 1962 it was found to be a sign of ozone's presence. Measurements taken in both aircraft showed concentrations of 0.065 ppmv and 0.12 ppmv.

As ozone is a strong respiratory irritant which can be toxic, exposure to the gas is regulated in industry and in the air. In the latter case, the maximum concentration permitted by the FAA is 0.25 ppmv at any time above 32,000 feet, or 0.1 ppmv for periods longer than three hours above 27,000 feet. The presence of ozone on board can be reduced through the installation of control equipment and/or through the avoidance of routes or altitudes where the gas is most prevalent. New aircraft, such as the Boeing 777, have catalytic converters with 98 percent efficiency to remove ozone as standard equipment. Some airlines, such as *Lufthansa*, have retrofitted their aircraft with ozone-dissociation apparatus.

Also see **Cabin Air Quality**.

PREGNANCY

A first officer on a Boeing 747–400 was told by her airline that she had to give up flying once her pregnancy had been declared. Although such advice is standard, it is not accurate. According to the International Commission on Radiological Protection (ICRP), she should limit her exposure to about 1 millisieverts (mSv) or the equivalent of about 200 flying hours during the remainder of her pregnancy. The actual radiation dose will depend on the routes and altitude flown.

Pregnant women, who in the past were confined at home

or expected to lead a sedentary existence, are more active today and travel for business and pleasure. Air travel, which is a convenient mode of transport for pursuing such plans, can be undertaken until the end of the 35th week. This stipulation varies slightly with different airlines, which are also likely to require a medical certificate that specifies the expected day of delivery. As a precautionary measure it is advised to check with the immigration regulations of the country to be visited, as some refuse entry to passengers in advanced stages of pregnancy.

On board, expectant mothers (as well as all other passengers) should take into consideration the various aspects of the cabin environment (*see* **Blood Circulation**, **Gas Expansion**, **Humidity** and **Radiation**).

1. In general, your water intake should be maintained and foods that produce intestinal gas should be avoided prior to a flight or on board. The resultant expansion of gases in the intestines can cause discomfort.
2. As pregnancy tends to increase the blood's viscosity, expectant mothers should try to be more active than usual on board. They should also request an aisle seat and spend 15 minutes each hour walking about.
3. Seat belts should be worn low around the pelvis.
4. Methods used to avoid jetlag should exclude drugs, focusing instead on sleep patterns and airline schedules (see **Jetlag**).
5. If there is an opportune time to fly First or Business Class, it is during pregnancy. Not only does the use of leg-rests encourage better circulation, but the less cramped and crowded conditions result in reduced fatigue and greater comfort.

6. Frequent flyers or aircrew need not cease flying but abide by the ICRP's recommendations.

PREMIUM CLASSES

> *General Norman Schwarzkopf, who has flown a lot during his illustrious military career including a record-breaking 23-hour nonstop flight from Karachi, Pakistan to Tampa, Florida, is clear on the issue of travel: "Economy might get you there cheaper," he says, "but you won't be fighting fit when you touch down."*

Even frequent flyers with little knowledge of aviation health have instinctively opted for Premium Class, a healthy way to fly.

There are several advantages that passengers gain in terms of their health when they fly the Premium Classes (First and Business Class), particularly First Class. In an indoor environment like an aircraft, a fixed volume of air is circulated every five to eight minutes. The factor that determines the amount each passenger obtains is the density per section, which is based on the seat configuration and load factor. As a result, the Premium Classes receive two to three times more air than Economy. In First Class, passengers can have between 40 and 60 cubic feet per minute, which allows for a more comfortable atmosphere than their fellow travelers' enjoy (*see* **Cabin Air Quality**).

One of the most important functions of an aircraft seat

is its facility to recline. The supine position is best for circulation of blood which, because of factors such as prolonged immobility and dry air, has a tendency to coagulate. Seats in Premium Classes enable the passenger to lower the backrest and raise the leg-rest to achieve an optimum posture for circulation (*see* **Airline Seats** and **Blood Circulation**).

Stress at airports is a well-known hazard of air travel. But the least stressed passengers are those who fly the Premium Classes, as there are various facilities on the ground to help alleviate anxiety. The most common is a special lounge, an oasis of calm for their use. In addition, some airlines, such as *Air France, Lufthansa, SAS, Swissair* and *British Airways*, provide check-in facilities at particular hotels or at a car-rental desk. Others, such as *Emirates, Continental* and *Virgin*, offer limousine service to the airport, while *Aer Lingus* offers this for passengers arriving at JFK (New York) and Logan (Boston). *Austrian Airlines*, which specializes in flights to Eastern Europe, offers not only a minimum connection time—half an hour—from Vienna to destinations further on, but also a limousine service once passengers arrive in Moscow, Odessa or Kiev. In Bucharest they provide free space in their Business Centre for Business Class or Travel Club members. Another service offered at airports is the Fast Track Lane (Heathrow and Gatwick) and INSpass (a combination smart ID card and palm print, available at JFK and Newark), to make departing and arriving quicker and easier.

Three airlines also offer a somewhat unusual service to Premium passengers. There is the world's first Arrivals Lounge at Terminal 4, Heathrow, where *British*

Airways passengers can shower and have their clothes pressed. *SAS* provide an efficient hotel check-in service on arrival at seven airports, including Stockholm, Oslo, Copenhagen and London, whereby a passenger collects his or her key while any luggage is delivered straight to the hotel, so the passenger can proceed directly to any meetings he or she has to attend. Among other benefits of its Priority Passenger Service (PPS), *Singapore Airlines* features free medical and personal accident cover as well as a guarantee to members of access to an Economy Class seat—provided 24 hours notice is given.

Each person requires a certain amount of personal space in order to feel safe and secure. This is a well-known phenomenon and is defined as **Safe Space**. It is of particular importance when we are exposed to strangers in crowded situations such as aircraft. The invasion of this private or intimate space during a flight can lead to irritation, annoyance and/or frustration and can culminate in rare instances of aggressive behaviour. It is easier to keep any intrusions at bay and preserve personal space in the comfortable setting of First or Business Class.

An essential element of air travel is that it can provide the passenger with quality time to relax, recuperate or sleep. In the Premium Classes passengers are treated as individuals and can eat, drink or be entertained whenever they desire. The seats are the most comfortable in the aircraft and are conducive to relaxation and sleep. This is a good prescription for the body, as it has to cope with various uncommon demands in the flight environment.

Wired

✈ John Thornton, who is a partner with the investment bankers Goldman Sachs, is a top flier amongst the partners, chalking up between 300,000 and 400,000 miles a year. Out of the 250 working days in a year he estimates that he can spend between 50 to 100 nights away. He has been flying for the past 15 years, since he joined the company at the age of 25. "I don't think twice about flying," he says. "For me, it's part of being alive. Travel, in the past decade, has become an essential feature of our industry. Until the beginning of the eighties, the world used to be the U.S. Now the world is the world."

In the early years of his career, adrenaline kept him going. But then two things happened to his health. The first concerned his digestive system. "It got screwed up," he recalls, "and my doctor warned me that I was getting an ulcer." The second symptom he experienced was that he was becoming fundamentally tired. Subsequently, he adopted several different strategies. "I never travel during the day," he comments. "I always travel at night and sleep on board. You could say my response is Pavlovian because whenever I'm on board I automatically go to sleep."

He never eats a meal in-flight or drinks anything except water. There is a danger of eating too much when he travels because of the time zone changes and the accessibility of airline food. In fact, he prefers to skip a meal rather than consume an extra one. With sleep, on the other hand, he finds that it is better to have more sleep than the normal quantity.

His body has now reached a plateau and has adjusted and functions well in this regime. But like most business flyers, his credo is "Time is Money" and he keeps a tight rein on it. Flying First Class is his safeguard against any problems. "I want to be able to control the glitches as much as possible," he says. "When I arrive at 10:25 for a 11:00 flight, I need to be whisked on board without much fuss."

His other countermeasures include loyalty to one airline, which for him is *British Airways*, and to be a member of an airline executive club. In his case, he wields a lot of influence with the airline as he is a holder of their top card. The privileges of the card and flying First Class enable him to obtain the support he needs. "My business is wired," he adds, "and an airline could be a weak link in the chain."

PRESSURE CABIN

It adds six tons in payload or the equivalent of the weight of 60 passengers to pressurize a Boeing 747–400.

Whenever we travel by air, the space we inhabit must be pressurized. The procedure is similar to blowing air into a balloon or using a bicycle pump to inflate a tire. The

pressure inside the cabin must be higher than that outside, because the outside pressure is so low that breathing would be impossible. The difference between the
two pressures, outside and inside an aircraft cabin, is
called the *cabin pressure differential.*

Piston-engined planes and turboprops have air com-
pressors to maintain a supply of pressurized air, while
the engines of jet airliners compress air as part of their
operation. The air, which is bled from each engine,
enters the fuselage throughout the flight to keep the
pressure constant. There are outflow valves to control
the expulsion of air and to protect the aircraft itself
from excessive differential pressures. (Such pressurization is essential: too great a difference in the outside
and inside pressures and, as in the case of the balloon
or bicycle tire, the plane would either burst or crumple
in on itself.)

There is a general belief that the pressure in the
cabin (or, as it is known, *cabin altitude*) is equivalent to
that at sea level. This is not the case. Cabin altitude can
fluctuate from 5,000 to 8,600 feet in cruise levels and is
dependent on many variables, including the load factor,
fuel burn, the aircraft's age and model and, above all,
the airline or captain's preference.

In the instance of an aircraft cruising at an altitude
below its operational ceiling, there is a choice. The pilot
can either select the maximum cabin differential pressure (about 5,000–6,000 feet) to increase the comfort of
the passengers, or make things easier on the cabin
structure (what is known as "prolonging the cabin's
fatigue life") by keeping the differential pressure at a
setting of around 8,000 feet.

The optimum cabin altitude for the 747–400 at flight

levels of 29,000–41,000 feet is 8,000 feet, according to Bob Fletcher, Head Flight Operations Engineer of *Air New Zealand*. The *Concorde* is an exception because its cabin altitude can be maintained at 5,000 feet due to its high cabin pressure differential (*see* **Concorde**).

The most obvious sign of pressurization on aircraft is the size and thickness of the windows. These are smaller than are found on surface transport. The largest civilian aircraft, the 747–400, has rectangular windows measuring 30 cm/12 in wide and 40 cm/16 in in diameter. There are three layers: an outer pane, an inner pane and a scratch pane on the passenger side. The first two panes are strengthened with laminates; they are made to withstand the pressure load pushing outwards from within the cabin.

If cabins of aircraft were pressurized to sea level, penalties for carrying too much fuselage weight and fuel would be incurred.

CABIN PRESSURE LOSS

The loss of cabin pressure during a flight, which is called decompression, is a rare occurrence. Going back to the analogy of the balloon, it would be as if there were either a gradual leak of air through the neck or a tiny hole, or a sudden outrush of air when the rubber bursts with a bang.

With a slow decompression, which usually results from a malfunction of the control system, the cabin altitude increases gradually. Few are aware of it until the altitude exceeds 10,000 feet, at which point a siren sounds and a warning light flashes in the cockpit. The pilot will take evasive action and descend to a lower flight level. At the same time, the "rubber jungle" descends in the cabin—the signal for the passengers to reach for their oxygen masks and breathe through them.

A rapid decompression, on the other hand, is immediately obvious because it occurs with an explosive noise when the fuselage ruptures. There is also a massive outrush of air which pulls and sucks everything close to the fracture or hole, as the pressure equalizes. The outside air is freezing cold and is accompanied by lower pressure, which causes instant hypoxia, or oxygen deficiency (*see* **Oxygen Deficiency**).

When a decompression occurs it is best to reach for the oxygen mask immediately. An investigation carried out into peoples' reactions to a decompression under simulated conditions revealed that up to 40 percent were either unprepared to don their masks, as they were involved in other activities, or took too long to do so. It is important to note that the mask has to be placed over your nose and face *immediately*, and that pulling on the lanyard initiates the flow of oxygen.

Once the mask is in place you are free to assist others such as children or passengers who are asleep. If no mask appears above your seat, ask a flight attendant for a portable oxygen canister. Although there is only a remote chance of a decompression occurring on a flight, forewarned is forearmed.

PROPERTIES OF AIR

The famous Cambridge physiologist, Sir Bryan Mathews, whose research made high-altitude flying possible, was once

*asked to sum up aviation medicine. He
answered in two words: "Boyle's Law."*

The seventeenth-century experiments of Robert Boyle,
who was the first scientist to study the properties of air,
are still relevant in the space age. The main apparatus
he used was an air pump which drew out air from a
glass chamber to which it was connected.

One of the first tasks he undertook was to test the
hypothesis of Galileo and others that air had weight. He
confirmed this by proving that exhausted chambers
were lighter than those containing air. Subsequent
experiments included placing various animals and
lighted candles into his improved exhaustion chamber,
or "pneumatical engine," as it was known.

One famous experiment involved placing a viper in
the pneumatical engine. Boyle noticed a bubble of gas
moving to and fro in one of the viper's eyes. This gas
bubble he observed was later recognized to be nitrogen,
the main cause of decompression sickness—a term
coined by Sir Bryan, who also categorized its various
symptoms such as "the bends," "the creeps," "the
chokes" and "the staggers" (*see* **Decompression
Sickness**).

Boyle's Law, the most important contribution he
made to the space age, governs the relationship
between man and his movement through the atmosphere. The Law states: "The volume of a gas varies
inversely with pressure at constant temperature." It
sounds complicated, but it means that gases (for example, those in the stomach) expand as a plane gains altitude, while outside air pressure decreases. This
explains why oxygen levels in the blood fall (there is

less air pressure)—and also why gases in any cavity or semicavity within the body increase when we fly.

RADIATION

Although everyone is exposed to radiation, including passengers in aircraft, there are some exceptions. These are smokers, heavy drinkers and people with certain cardiovascular and respiratory conditions whose "normally" high level of oxygen deficiency makes them resistant to its effects.

The earth is exposed to streams of radiation from outer space and from the sun—these are called cosmic rays. Though a substantial proportion is absorbed in the upper layer of the atmosphere, some still penetrate to ground level where they form part of the natural environment.

There are two main sources of radiation: natural (which constitutes 87 percent) and man-made (some 13 percent). (*See* Table 11 in Appendix A.) The average annual dose per person in the U.K. is 2.6 millisieverts (mSv).

The intensity of cosmic radiation increases with altitude because the atmosphere becomes thinner and less able to absorb it. High-altitude flight elevates the degree of exposure, which can rise from 100 to 300 times that of sea level. The *Concorde*, at a cruise level of 60,000 feet, has a dose rate per hour twice that of a subsonic aircraft such as a Boeing 747 which operates at over

35,000 feet. But then it flies at least twice as fast, so the radiation exposure for both aircraft is about the same.

The radiation dose on average per hour at sea level is 0.03 microsieverts, compared with 4 microsieverts on short-haul flights, 5 microsieverts on long-haul flights and over 10 microsieverts on *Concorde* (1,000 microsieverts = 1 millisievert). Unlike subsonic aircraft, the *Concorde* is equipped with a warning system in case this level of radiation exposure is exceeded, particularly in a year of high solar activity. In the instance of amber or red alerts, 100 to 500 microsieverts would be recorded and a descent initiated. (This has never happened on *Concorde* over the past 20 years.)

Latitude is another factor in exposure to cosmic radiation: there is 50 percent less radiation at the equator than at the poles.

The U.K.'s National Radiological Protection Board (NRPB) estimates that commercial aircrews receive an extra 2 mSv per year by virtue of their occupation. This brings their total to 4.6 mSv, which places them in the group of occupationally exposed workers.

According to the NRPB, frequent flyers (taking between five and six transatlantic trips per year) receive a slightly higher dose rate of 0.4 mSv than the annual average of the U.K. population. The dose rate for some frequent flyers could be nearer 1 mSv a year. In flying time, this represents about 200 hours in a subsonic aircraft or 100 hours in a *Concorde*. This additional exposure is still within the recommended limit set by the International Commission on Radiation Protection (ICRP) in 1991 for members of the public. Aircrew, too, are within the ICRP's recommended limit of 20 mSv for occupational exposure.

As radiation results in the production of free radicals—highly reactive molecules created in the body from exposure to exhausts and other environmental pollutants and also a by-product of the body's normal metabolism—it is important to know about methods of reducing their effects:

- Drinking red wine regularly is a pleasurable mode of protection. A Cabernet Sauvignon is favoured because it contains high concentrations of the grape pigment, enoviton, which has been found by Bulgarian scientists to be helpful to people recovering from radiation sickness. They claim that enoviton stimulates the body to eliminate radioactive substances and ensures that the immune system is able to counter the after-effects of radiation exposure. However, the only drawback to this remedy is that you may need to drink a lot (post-flight) for it to be effective.

- Vitamins C and E are scavengers of free radicals. Unlike enoviton, you need only take normal supplements to reap the benefits.

SAFE SPACE

The configurations of seats on aircraft must surely rank as the most efficient use of space in the modern world. There is enough room for up to 400 people on the wide-bodied Boeing 747–400. Yet, could such an enclosed area be designated as over-crowded?

A wide variety of animals, from sticklebacks, canaries and rats to deer and lions, mark out a piece of territory which they regard as theirs, and defend it fiercely. This is their *safe space*. The same principle applies to human beings, except that a greater number of subtleties are involved. For most people, safe space is essentially an area around them within which they feel at ease and secure, protected from outside intrusion whether in the form of excessive sensory stimuli or interaction with others. It is also an environment where stress is kept to a minimum.

Our sense of space and distance is not static, however, and does not end with our skin. There are four distance zones around each person: intimate (encompassing a circle of 1.5 feet), personal (up to 4 feet), social (up to 8 feet) and public (a circle of up to 40 feet). Each zone is delineated by your senses as well as by physical gestures and/or verbal cues that bring others closer or keep them away, such as shaking your fist in another's face, keeping someone "at arm's length," or encouraging another to enter your intimate space with the words "I love you."

The space which concerns air travelers does not fit into any of these categories. It overlaps all of them and as such could be termed public/intimate space. This is similar to the situation of sailors on a submarine, where crew members live and work at close quarters yet in a strictly formal atmosphere.

The best description for this public/intimate zone around airline passengers, though, is safe space. Maintaining this space is a protective mechanism. It prevents people from fighting each other in over-crowded situations. The body and the immediate area surrounding it are considered sacrosanct and any intruders are regarded as a threat which could provoke anxiety or stress. Within this safe space people feel at ease and secure.

A significant function of this space is to keep outside stimulation to an acceptable level and avoid extreme sensory input or interactions with others which may in themselves be harmful to our health. In specific circumstances—on a crowded bus, for example—these intrusions cannot be prevented and we adopt defensive rituals and postures to counter them. The avoidance of eye or body contact are examples. Sometimes encounters with strangers will produce a high degree of anxiety and arouse the "fight or flight" response (*see* **Stress**). This could result in aggression.

We need to be alone and enjoy privacy just as much as we need to be close and intimate with others. When these requirements are fulfilled, it induces feelings of warmth and security within our safe space. This is reflected physiologically and can result in a reduction of stress hormones, a slower heart beat and even the secretion of endorphins, which produce sensations of tranquility.

The feeling of overcrowdedness does occasionally arise on board a plane, for example when a group of people such as a press corps, a large family or a sports team are traveling together. They know each other so well that it is difficult for other passengers to make them understand that an unacceptable level of intrusion has been reached. It is at this stage when, deprived of privacy, arguments and friction can arise between passengers. Robert Redford greatly values his privacy and in Utah, where he lives, he spent over $2 million buying up a plot of land next to his ranch to separate himself farther from his neighbors. On air trips, it is customary for him to buy two First Class seats next to each other in order to protect his safe space. If he did not take that course of action he would feel he was impelled to give a performance to his fellow passenger.

The most obvious center of safe space on an aircraft is your seat. In the Premium Classes, particularly First Class, a sense of inner well-being can easily be achieved because of the ample room provided. Service is also likely to be flexible and you can work, relax or sleep with a minimum of disturbance. It is more challenging to protect your safe space in Economy Class because of the high levels of intrusion and the lack of room.

The key to achieving an effective safe space is to spread yourself and take possession of as much space around you as you can, including any empty seats nearby. Consequently, you extend your safe space.

The first step is to fill the seat pouch in front of you. You can immediately double your area if you travel with a member of your family or choose to make contact with fellow passengers. But you may prefer to limit communication with your fellow passengers and adopt defensive postures such as the avoidance of eye contact.

Another technique is to exercise your right to do whatever you like within your space. You may want to stretch your arms or legs to encourage circulation (see **Exercise**), or perhaps counter the effects of the cabin environment by applying rehydration gel, a cooling eye compress or a facial spray. On the other hand, if you fly the Premium Classes of certain airlines, such as *British Airways*, they not only have videos of suitable exercises but also provide passengers with products for neutralizing the dry air. Such rituals are an essential part of engendering ease and well-being, and should be carried out throughout your trip.

Two further strategies can be employed. You may wish to bring with you some items from home that will give you peace of mind, such as your own pillow, a teddy bear or even a favorite snack. The simplest approach is to retreat within your safe space and go to sleep. At a stroke you can block out all intrusions—provided you use earplugs and an eye mask. For a total retreat you may consider covering your head with a blanket. This has the additional advantages of limiting your water loss and keeping you warm.

SEA-LEVEL OPTION

> *King Khaled of Saudi Arabia converted the upper deck of his personal 747 into an operating room and always travels with a medical team in case of emergency—he has a heart condition. Had he known that it was possible to fly in a jet while maintaining the ideal conditions of sea level inside, he could have dispensed with all the costly medical equipment and personnel.*

For a billionaire, sea-level flying is always an option. Whenever aeronautical engineers have been asked whether it is possible to design a jet aircraft that could provide the cabin atmosphere of sea level even at high cruising altitudes, their main objection has been that the fuselage would have to be so heavy that the plane could not operate efficiently.

A short study carried out by British Aerospace Airbus identified the two principal effects of modifying cabin altitude in this way: an increase in both the weight of the fuselage and the amount of fuel needed (known technically as the fuselage weight penalty and fuel penalty respectively—*see* Table 12 in Appendix A).

This study showed, however, that these increases were only moderate: 6 percent fuselage penalty/4,000 pounds more fuel in the case of the Boeing 747–400; 5.8 percent/100 pounds more fuel for the BAe 146 or Whispering Jet; and 5.2 percent/60 pounds more fuel for the Gulfstream IV, provided that each aircraft was flown to the maximum of its range.

Although the costs of converting the cabins to sea level at cruise may seem from these results to be small, there is another factor that has not yet been considered (and this is where the billionaire comes in!): The actual cost of the conversion would be equivalent to the price of a new aircraft, or even more. The two smaller jets (the BAe 146 and the Gulfstream IV) can be taken as examples of the expenditure involved. They cost about $24 million each. The price of "the sea-level option," including the conversion kit, labour (estimated at 100,000–200,000 man-hours) and nonrecurring expenses such as the design, flight test, etc., could well come to $36.6 million—minimum. The total, therefore, for the privilege of flying in an optimum atmosphere would be about $60 million. For an even smaller jet, such as the Cessna Citation, the overall cost would be about $17 million.

There are two alternative ways of achieving a similar effect without paying such a vast sum. The first is to fly at a lower altitude: because of the cabin pressure differential, the cabin altitude would decrease accordingly (*see* **Pressure Cabin**). The only penalty would be the increased cost of fuel, but you would never attain sea-level atmosphere in the cabin. The other method is to incorporate such a feature into the design of a new aircraft before its construction. Consequently, all passengers on this aircraft would enjoy the health bonus for only slightly more money, to cover the fuselage weight and fuel penalties. And it is possible that such an aircraft will be designed in the not-too-distant future.

SEX

"One of the problems cabin crew have to deal with is sex," says Robert Hubbard of Delta Air Lines. Although only a small number of these "incidents" occur, it is a fact of life on board. It has been observed in a cross-section of passengers, from teenagers to the elderly—they become overwhelmed by sudden amorousness during a flight. The policy of most airlines is to exercise discretion in such situations; ultimately it is the flight attendant who decides whether to ask the couple to desist or to smother them with blankets.

The existence of the "Mile High Club" is the result of a number of variables. The most obvious is that travel causes dislocations. Passengers are away from the social constraints of families and friends, and one study showed that women, in particular, are affected by this. A trip on an aircraft is the beginning of being on one's own and, for some, gives them the feeling of freedom to do as they wish.

Anxiety, too, is part of the picture. Contrary to popular belief, it does not inhibit sexual arousal. In terms of aerophobia, therefore, some people seek to put their fear out of their minds by engaging in sex. This is not uncommon.

An aphrodisiac is always present on board, in the form of cerebral hypoxia (oxygen deficiency) caused by the lower pressure of the cabin. Other elements that can contribute to lack of oxygen to the brain (and the light-headedness or slight intoxication this can produce) include drinking alcohol, taking certain medications (such as amyl nitrates, used in the treatment of angina pectoris), smoking and the presence of certain medical conditions such as chronic lung or heart disease. A mixture of alcohol and drugs such as antidepressants (prothiadom) under such circumstances can put a passenger into a particularly heavy-duty state of hypomania—the main characteristic of which is sexual disinhibition.

Although it would be difficult to provide a profile of a typical member of this club, there are two likely candidates. The first is somewhat immature emotionally, taking part out of sheer bravado and so that he or she can boast about it later. The other is inclined to be anxious and compensates for this with sexual activity.

There was a celebrated incident of a few years ago (which only came to light because the matter went to court) in which a woman flight attendant (who was off-duty at the time) was involved in sexual misconduct with two passengers and a crew member. As it turned out, she had taken antidepressants during the trip and had consumed several glasses of champagne.

SLEEP

Sleep disruption caused by jetlag is a common experience among most passengers, even frequent flyers. Judy Moon of Delta Air Lines, who has worked as a flight attendant for 25 years, has a perfect solution: she eats crackers. "Whenever I wake up at 2 A.M. in a hotel or at home," she says, "and can't go back to sleep, I eat something light like a piece of bread or crackers. I never touch protein. And I go back to sleep without fail."

Sleep, which leads to the restoration of the body's energy, is the best antidote against the less positive effects of air travel (*see* **Jetlag**). Passengers who cannot sleep on board may want to build up "sleep credits" prior to departure. Essentially, if you normally sleep eight hours, by getting slightly more than this in the days before you fly you will be "in credit."

On the other hand, there will be a proportional decrease in how long you can stay wakeful if your sleep is reduced to less than you normally get in the days before you depart. As a result, a sleep deficit will be registered. Passengers can add to their sleep store by having a nap (of an hour or more) before they take off. Another method is to gear yourself up to your new time zone several days before your flight by going to sleep either earlier each evening (if you are going to be traveling east) or later (if journeying west).

There are some useful techniques for inducing sleep. Some flight attendants swear by taking an aspirin before bedtime. A sleep research laboratory in the U.K. has discovered two novel ways of promoting sleep. The first is to warm the brain slightly during the day, for example, by sitting under a hair dryer. There are other means of obtaining the same results, such as taking a warm bath, lying quietly in a warm room or exercising. The second solution is to increase your brain's "visual load" by window-shopping, sightseeing or visiting an art gallery for an hour or two before you fly or once you land. Watching television or a film, unless it's on a wide screen at a cinema, will not work as the colors and/or dimensions are not complex enough to get your brain going.

The obvious way of adapting the first method on board is to wear a woollen cap or balaclava. The latter would also serve as an excellent safeguard against moisture loss.

A final suggestion about sleeping on an aircraft is to upgrade to Business Class or First. Ian Webster, Senior Manager Relationships Marketing at *British Airways*, offers by way of illustration an event that happens often on flights throughout the world:

A business group goes on a conference to, say, Toronto from the U.K., and returns on a night flight a couple of days later. As the aircraft is full, they are spread between the three cabins. On arrival the next morning the senior executives (who were in First) go straight back to work, those in middle management (who were in Business) return to their offices at lunch time, and the junior staff (who were placed in Economy) come in the next day (see **Premium Classes**).

Swissair provides their transit passengers with beds at Swiss airports if they have to wait for four fours or more for a connecting flight. This unique service is offered to all passengers, regardless of the cost of their ticket.

Whenever James Bond, a.k.a. Pierce Brosnan, flies he travels in Coach but always manages to arrive looking good. His secret is to get the studio to buy four seats together so that he can sleep comfortably throughout the trip.

TV personality Anneka Rice set a new around-the-world record in 43 hours, 43 minutes by scheduled aircraft. A key element in achieving this was the fact that she took along a goosedown pillow which enabled her to sleep on board.

Automatic Sleep Pilot

✈ An original method for sleeping on aircraft has been advised by a *British Airways* 747–400 Senior First Officer, Ann Peacock.

"It was a desperate measure," she says, "as I find it difficult to sleep, particularly during the day while I'm on my three-hour rest break." The long-range aircraft that she flies on has two bunks behind the cockpit for use by both relief and operational crew. This is necessary as the flight can vary from nine to 15 hours.

"One day, I finally managed to nod off and I have had no trouble since. The technique I use is what I describe as modified self-hypnosis. I lie on the bunk with my eyes closed and begin breathing in and out slowly for a period of four seconds. I repeat this for three or four times as it relaxes me.

"Then I start to recall a story of a book I've read. It's not just any book as it can't be too exciting or horrifying. That produces bad dreams. But one you can't put down once you've started. It usually has a plot that is very involved. A good example is Dick Francis or *The Golden Deed* by Andrew Garve.

"This routine has worked so well that now I simply lie in the bunk and I go to sleep. Sometimes I have to repeat a story but mostly I just make a note of the time I need to wake and I'm asleep."

STOPOVERS

I'm not afraid of flying, I'm afraid of arriving.
HELENE HANFF, *84 CHARING CROSS ROAD*

Nonstop flights, which save us the time and trouble of interconnections on the ground, are popular in intercontinental travel. But as these flights make additional demands on the body and mind, passengers in Economy Class may benefit from stopovers. At a simple level, they should fly during the day and spend the evening at a hotel. A night at the Pierre, in New York, for example, where the guest is cossetted with goosedown pillows, silky Frette sheets and a soft bed, is incomparable to the extra hours spent in cramped quarters on board. They wake refreshed, perhaps take in some sightseeing and continue their trip.

Long-distance flights can be turned into pleasurable events much the same way as cruises can when stopovers with interesting sights and hotels are included in the itinerary. One of the masters of this game is the British fashion designer Sir Hardy Amies. He spreads a nonstop trip of 26 hours over ten days. Each stopover is calculated to prolong his enjoyment. "My favorite long-haul journey, which I have made frequently over the years, is to Sydney, Australia." He enhances his pleasure by flying with different airlines across various sectors, using *Concorde* on the first leg from London to New York. He spends a week in New York before taking a day flight to Los Angeles. Whenever possible he chooses a carrier that serves his preferred delicacy, caviar.

Sir Hardy finds L.A. a good stopover destination, for it has Disneyland and Hollywood—and its well-kept secret, Redondo Beach. Located only seven miles south of the airport, this scenic location has not only an excellent beach and marina with the Crowne Plaza Hotels and Resorts situated next to it, but also 18 miles of coastal trails for biking, jogging, roller-skating and walking.

Once in Sydney, Sir Hardy stays at the Sebel Town House "which," he comments, "is like staying with friends. But of course, friends are better because they are cheaper." Another hotel recommended for Sydney's King's Cross area is the Nikko, which offers superb harbor views.

A stopover is not only an innovative way to travel which can prolong the pleasure of a trip but also provides a bonus in terms of a passenger's physiological and psychological well-being. Even businessmen can benefit after a successful tour by spending the odd night somewhere. "During the two decades I flew intensively," says Sir Peter Walters, the top British industrialist, "I would always stop for a game of golf in Singapore. Otherwise, I would be like a tiger pacing a cage."

Iceland, for example, is an ideal layover on the busy North Atlantic route, as everything in the country is special—from its natural light, its hot springs and unusual horses, which move at a unique pace, to the variety of sports including jet-skiing, fishing and golf, even at midnight during the summer. *Icelandair* has excellent connections to and from Europe and the USA and offers complimentary stopovers to full-fare Business Class passengers. Airlines, such as *Qantas, Emirates* and *Cathay Pacific*, also encourage passengers to break up their long-haul flights with stops, and offer special excursions at destinations along the way.

Some people who are particularly sensitive to the lower cabin pressure during intercontinental travel would also gain from stopovers. These include the elderly, people with chronic obstructive lung disease or asthma, highly trained athletes, smokers and those who are overweight.

STRESS

"Airport strain is what's exhausting," says Anthony Sampson, author of **Empires of the Skies**. *He prefers to fly from a regional airport rather than a major hub.*

The stress air travelers encounter is dissimilar to any other experienced in surface forms of transport. It is the flight itself which presents numerous physiological challenges unique to aviation. These include oxygen deficiency, dehydration, gas expansion, time zone changes, prolonged sitting and exposure to environmental tobacco smoke. There is also the availability of alcohol (which increases oxygen lack and the likelihood of jetlag) and the anxiety some passengers feel about air travel.

Irrespective of whether it is caused by anxiety or aggression, stress increases the total concentration in the bloodstream of the stress hormones *adrenaline* and *noradrenaline*. The noradrenaline level is raised more by anxiety-stress, such as when we are anxious about flying or about what awaits us at our destination; the adrenaline level is elevated more by aggressive circumstances such as when we have to cope with crowds or traffic.

Conditions which are distinguished by novelty, anticipation, unpredictability and change produce a rise in adrenaline, too. The adrenaline level will fall, however, if we gain control over the situation. Nevertheless, both hormones stimulate activity that will elevate blood glucose concentrations and fatty acids. This ensures the ready availability of fuels for the "fight or flight" response to stress situations.

Modern man, unlike primitive man, is unlikely to exercise after a stress situation. Therefore, the fuel concentrations remain high for prolonged periods.

Such a failure to oxidize the glucose and fatty acids can, in the long term (and particularly in obese or unfit individuals), lead to the development of a degenerative disease of the arteries called atherosclerosis. This condition is characterized by deposits of fatty material on the lining of the arteries.

The best method of reducing stress in the flight environment is to gain a measure of control over your situation. This will immediately result in a decrease in the secretion of stress hormones. There are two main sources of stress: the airport and the aircraft.

The first step in reducing stress on the ground is to allow yourself sufficient time to check in, at least an hour before a domestic or short-haul flight, and some two hours before an international flight. Remember that airports are crowded places with queues, long distances to walk, immigration controls, security checks and the inevitable flight delays. Once you have allocated an appropriate amount of time for departure, you can fill the interval to your best advantage by following these tips:

1. Ensure that you exercise, to consume the energy that has accumulated through the stress hormone secretions. Brisk walking along the concourse will suffice.
2. Relax your mind, either by reading an interesting book or dealing with a backlog of work.
3. Reduce the weight of your hand luggage by checking in more for the cargo hold and keeping only essential items.
4. Elderly or overweight passengers, or those with serious heart conditions, should ensure that ground transport is available. Notify airline staff on arrival.
5. Communicate with other passengers if you find that you are edgy or tense. This can help diffuse your feelings.

6. Use the airline Club Lounge. This is a quiet haven in the turbulent environment of an airport. At Kai Tak Airport, Hong Kong, *Cathay Pacific* provides electronic massage chairs, showers, and sleeper sofas.

7. One solution is to fly from an uncongested airport. In the U.K., there is the London City Airport (which has a 15-minute check-in), or Stansted. *KLM* operates a unique service of "feeder flights" from regional airports like Aberdeen, Edinburgh, Teesside, Leeds/Bradford and Cardiff to Schipol. There, connecting flights with minimum waiting periods of 40 to 50 minutes take off for European and intercontinental destinations.

8. If you are flying out of Switzerland, make use of their Fly Baggage and rail station check-in systems:

    Operated from 117 train or "postbus" stations, Fly Baggage allows you to check your luggage right through to your final destination. It is available to passengers of all airlines except *British Airways*, *Air Lanka*, *City Express*, and all U.S. carriers.

    The rail station check-in, available at 24 major centres in Switzerland, enables passengers to obtain boarding cards from 2 to 24 hours prior to departure. *Swissair*, *Delta Air Lines*, *SAS*, *Singapore* and *Austrian* are the only airlines with access to this scheme.

    You can also use a scheme of this kind if you are flying to Switzerland, whereby your luggage can be checked right through to your final Swiss destination no matter how many connecting flights you have to make.

On board, there are various ways to keep stress at bay:

1. Distract yourself with interesting or light reading

material, the film, music channels, conversation or by focusing on activities planned at your destination.

2. When flight attendants bring round hot towels, use them in a unique way. A flight attendant from *Delta Air Lines* suggests that you should place it at the nape of your neck to release tension.

3. Avoid eating chocolates, soft cheeses, citrus fruits or yeast extract, and do not drink red wine—each of these can cause hypertension because they introduce tyramines into your system, which prevent glucose in the blood from being synthesized.

4. In First Class on *JAL*, a massage chair is provided for passengers. In Japan, such a facility is common in hotels and in waiting rooms of hospitals and companies.

Familiarity Breeds Less Stress

✈ Middleton Murray is a partner in the top Washington law firm Patton, Boggs and Blow. Now in his sixties, he has been traveling since his twenties when he worked for the U.S. government.

"The older you become," he says, "the more difficult it is to deal with jetlag. Whenever I fly across the Atlantic I take *Concorde* as it significantly reduces jetlag symptoms."

He has, however, developed an ingenious method to reduce travel stress. It is called familiarity. Whenever he goes on a trip he attempts to limit new experiences. "I fly on the same airline," he explains. "I have a fixed seat number on an aircraft, e.g., 2E on a B-767. I stay in the same hotel and eat in the same restaurant. The sense of doing the same things helps me to cope better with the stress."

SUPPLEMENTAL OXYGEN

Oxygen is the elixir of most problems encountered on board; in a survey of medical incidents it was found to be effective in 60 percent of cases.

Airlines are required by civil aviation authorities to carry oxygen supplies in the event of an emergency such as a decompression (*see* **Pressure Cabin**). The supplies are in the form of drop-down masks and portable oxygen canisters. The latter, which are for passenger use, each contain a sufficient quantity of the gas (120 litres) to allow either a 30-minute high flow or a 60-minute low flow. The number of units on board varies according to the aircraft model and the seat configurations. A typical example taken from the *British Airways* fleet is listed in Table 13, Appendix A.

In particular, passengers with stable medical conditions, blood disorders such as anaemia or sickle cell disease, or those who are recovering from illness may require supplemental oxygen on board (*see* **Medical Kits**).

Delta Air Lines, which offers a pre-flight medical screening for such passengers, found that 80 percent required or requested in-flight oxygen. The customer service department of the airline routinely refers air travelers with known medical conditions, needs or uncertain health status to its 24-hour medical advisory service for evaluation. An analysis of pre-flight screenings found that this service was worthwhile in the planning of safe, comfortable flights, since commercial air travel poses environmental and nonenvironmental stresses for such passengers.

Although on-board oxygen is available for medical incidents, the airline should be notified at least 48 hours before departure for any supplemental requirements, particularly for continuous oxygen throughout the flight. Most of the airlines charge a supplement for providing these additional facilities, which in the case of U.S. carriers can vary from U.S.$40 to U.S.$200. *Air Canada*, which offers a special oxygen medipak, has found that most requests for such a service come from people with sickle-cell anemia.

Your doctor should alert the medical department of the airline beforehand of your particular requirements. He or she may be asked to supply a written prescription and complete an INCAD form, which is the standard requisition form used by the International Air Transport Association (IATA).

THIRST

Water is best.
PINDAR, SIXTH-CENTURY B.C. GREEK POET

There is an insidious aspect of air travel which is analogous to mountaineering. It is the lack of the sensation of thirst. Water loss caused by breathing is great because of the absolute dryness of the air on board, and it is unusual to see sweat forming at high altitude, because moisture is rapidly removed by evaporation as it is formed.

There is evidence that dehydration resulting from rapid fluid loss while airborne does not trigger as strong a sensation of thirst as it does at sea level. This is due to the depressant action of the body's chemo-receptors when exposed to low oxygen pressure (*see* **Oxygen Deficiency**). This accounts for the positive disinclination of long-haul passengers to drink large amounts of fluid during their flight—they simply do not realize they are dehydrated.

The obvious way of bypassing this problem is to become superhydrated in advance of the flight. However, people are not camels. They neither have the capacity to drink over 30 percent of their body weight in one session nor to forgo water for periods of two weeks at a time.

If a passenger attempted to over-drink before a flight, the body would simply excrete any excess soon after boarding. The amount of water that can be stored in the body is a small fraction what we need. Of our blood volume of 5.5 litres, some 3.5 litres is plasma water, vital for circulation to function well.

Man has evolved drinking habits which, in temperate climates, result in his consumption of more water than is necessary to maintain the normal 50 to 60 percent of total body weight. In the desert, on the other hand, when sweating is profuse, the amounts of water drunk may be inadequate to replace the losses, and no amount of added sugar or salt can make much difference. The usual pattern is that a person drinks about half of what they need and then takes the remainder when they eat a meal.

As exposure to hypoxia (lack of oxygen) causes a reduction in spontaneous and induced water intake, it is essential to keep well hydrated on long-haul flights, particularly when the passenger load factor is low (see **Humidity**). On average, drinking a cupful of water every hour is enough—if the flight is full, about 20 percent less than this is needed. Besides drinking flat mineral water, rather than the gaseous version, eating green vegetables is a good source of fluid as they contain 90 to 97 percent moisture. Another method is to reduce the body's water requirement by avoiding diuretics such as alcohol, tea and coffee.

Passengers with renal or cardiovascular disease or those receiving vasopression therapy could be at risk if they take excessive amounts of water. The elderly too, particularly men with prostate conditions (whose bladders fill rapidly) should be careful about drinking large quantities of water. On a short flight it is better to become a bit dehydrated than to risk problems of urinary obstruction.

Children, who are more sensitive to water loss than adults, should be given small amounts at more frequent intervals (see **Children**).

Among the symptoms of discomfort that passengers experience from the lack of water on board are dryness of the eyes, nose and throat, nosebleeds and, among frequent flyers over the long term, urinary gravel.

Air Canada is one of the airlines that provides all the Executive First passengers with a 500 milliliter bottle of flat, mineral water after take-off.

WOMEN

A female journalist who works for a national newspaper and travels a lot in the U.S. complains about the treatment she receives from hoteliers as a single woman. She always seems to end up with the odd room in the hotel, particularly when she checks in with a female receptionist. She gets the one with the leaky faucet or near the elevator, which is usually allotted to families who would never kick up a fuss. However, she reappears at the reception area and quietly asks for another room. She always wins in the end.

There are several other aspects of flying which are of interest to women.

1. Water retention: Angela Rossi, an art dealer, uses an herbal diuretic whenever she flies. Another method, according to Vicki Bramwell, a journalist, is to exercise off the excess water. She goes for a gentle jog or swim postflight as she prefers not to use chemicals in her body.
2. Menstruation: It is common for women to either miss their periods when they fly a lot or to suffer from heavy periods. As air travel can disrupt the menstrual cycle, it is best to always be prepared. "I was in the middle of my cycle," says bestselling author, Rosalind Miles, "but when I arrived at my destination I had my period. As I had a problem finding tampons even in

shops in five-star hotels, I always take them with me."
For regular periods, *Lufthansa* purser Christine
Behmer recommends a high-dose pill as the low-dose
is ineffective.

3. Constipation: As the metabolism tends to slow down
   on long-haul flights, some female frequent flyers take
   along laxatives such as tybogel. Kiwi fruit is also effective.

4. Nail repair kits: Women with long nails tend to find
   that flying causes brittleness and they might tear, flake
   or break easily. It is recommended that a nail repair
   kit containing Krazy Glue be put into a travel kit.

5. Homeopathy and aromatherapy: Marguerite Littman,
   founder of the AIDS Crisis Trust, always travels with
   aromatherapy oils such as lavender which she pats
   around her neck and nasal area to ward off infection
   such as colds. It contains a natural antiseptic and
   antibiotic, and was used as a disinfectant for hospital
   floors in the past.

6. Diet: A long-haul flight is an ideal time to begin a fast
   or diet. Marie Helvin, international model, goes on a
   detox diet whenever she flies. She only eats one kind
   of fruit and drinks a lot of water. "It helps me to beat
   jetlag," she says.

7. Beauty treatment: Some female travelers give themselves a facial on board the aircraft. They make sure
   that they get a window seat so they can face away
   from fellow passengers and apply their creams and
   gauze in semiprivacy. "I survive long-haul trips," says
   Tracey Ullman, "through using lots and lots of mois-
   turizer."

THE WONDER JUICE

The wonder juice for air travelers was dis-
covered some 60 years ago by Dr. J. Argyll
Campbell, a prominent physiologist whose
work was largely ignored by the medical
establishment because of its focus on diet
(rather than drugs) to treat disease.

No, it is not one of those designer drinks that contain
mixtures of fruit and herbs, ginseng or guarana. It is
made with that most humble of root vegetables, the
carrot.

Carrots offer the best resistance to oxygen deficiency
(*see* **Oxygen Deficiency**). They were first issued to
pilots during the Second World War to promote their
night vision.

Dr Campbell, working during the 1930s, carried out
experiments on animals to find a substance that
would alleviate oxygen lack (hypoxia) in patients. His
no-nonsense method allowed him to conduct a large
number of investigations over a brief period of time. His
subjects were white rats upon whom he imposed a
severe but efficient test, the likes of which would not be
possible today. Several groups of rats were fed a variety
of diets including horsemeat (raw or cooked), milk, fish
(tinned salmon), fresh liver, cheese, vitamins and vegetables over a period of two to six days.

Subsequently, each group of animals was placed in a
small decompression or pressure chamber where the
temperature was kept at a constant heat of 33°C/91.4°F.
Within five minutes the pressure was reduced to 245
mmHg. This is equivalent to shooting to 28,000 feet, the

altitude of the Lhotse Face on Mount Everest, at a speed faster than the climbing rate of *Concorde*.

The benchmark for the experiment was based on the fact that those animals who had been fed a mixed diet died after about 10 minutes. Over a series of experiments, the vegetable that outperformed all other nutrients in terms of providing protection against the acute oxygen deficiency was the carrot. There was a 100 percent survival rate after 35 minutes. Without doubt, Dr. Campbell had proved that a diet of pure carrots increases resistance to oxygen lack.

A couple of interesting findings of the experiments are that boiling carrots does not lower their protective power, whereas taking large doses of carotene (the main nutrient in carrots) has little effect on increasing resistance to hypoxia.

Recent research on carotenoids, which are red or yellow pigments found in carrots and some other plants, shows that they protect against free radical damage mainly at relatively low oxygen pressures.

As the whole carrot is needed to achieve the desired effect, you cannot take the short-cut of taking vitamins or beta-carotene supplements.

Carrot juice is the most concentrated form of this root vegetable. Start a day or two prior to the flight. It is also effective if some 500 mililiter is consumed before take-off or during the flight.

(I should mention that carrot juice is not always easy to find abroad. If you cannot find it in any of the markets or shops, try your hotel. Once when I was at the Regent Hotel in Auckland, New Zealand, I realized some 20 minutes before check-out time that I had forgotten to buy some. In a panic I phoned room service, who within 10 minutes produced freshly squeezed carrot juice in a screw-top jar. I have been forever grateful.)

One alternative to drinking carrot juice is to eat as many carrots as you can stand two to three days prior to your flight. The virtue is that there are many ways carrots can be prepared, such as by boiling, steaming or baking them, or by using them in soups or cakes.

All Nippon Airways (ANA) is the first airline to introduce organic carrot juice in their First Class in all flights from Tokyo to Europe and the U.S. So you can sit back and your glass will be filled with C.J. without your even asking because their service is proactive.

Three

ENJOY YOUR FLIGHT!

*Anyone concerned with the motivation of travel
has to realize that he is reaching deep into one
of the conflicts of the human mind: a desire for
sameness, the return to the womb, if you wish;
conflicting with the motivation to reach out and
discover the world. In a sublimated fashion, a
trip is therefore a form of birth or rebirth.*

DR. ERNST DICHTER

Flying is a paradox. Although it is the safest form of
transport (a person is 25 times safer in an aircraft than
in a car, according to the international insurers Lloyds
of London), there are still people who are apprehensive
about air travel—including professional pilots and frequent flyers who, out of the blue, get the notion that
their "number might be up" on the next flight.

The origins of this paradox lie deep within the sub-
conscious. We are all born with an instinctive fear of
heights. Infants are routinely tested for the presence of
the Moro reflex, a grasping response to any stimulus
that simulates falling. As children grow up and gain

mastery over their environment, they learn which heights are safe and how to protect themselves from falling. There always remains, however, a link in our minds between heights and danger.

This fear has deep roots and is paradoxically associated with another emotion, joy. The joy of flying, which embodies the realization of humanity's dream of flight, provides the flyer with a sensation of power, control and freedom. It represents a triumph over the fear of heights which is analogous to a mountaineer's conquest of a peak. To some flyers, the ecstasies of flight exceed even this—in the words of American pilot and poet John Gillespie Magee in the final lines of his sonnet "High Flight," *"Put out my hand and touched the face of God."*

Such an act, which is presented as the ultimate expression of the joy of flight and frequently inscribed on plaques given as mementos to military flyers, is not only one of intimacy but of dominance. In psychodynamic terms this ascendancy over the Lord could be equivalent to having power over death.

The relationship between the twin emotions of the fear of heights (associated in our minds with the fatal consequences of falling) and the joy of flight (derived from the power of conquering the skies) reaches our most primitive depths. The ancient Greek myth of Daedalus and Icarus is one example of the profound nature of this relationship.

Daedalus, whose name is derived from the Greek for "cunning worker," was an Athenian architect and master craftsman who served King Minos of Crete. Among his many creations was the labyrinth at Knossos, in which the fearsome Minotaur was concealed. Later, he displeased the king and together with his son, Icarus, was confined to the maze. Their subsequent escape from imprisonment, flying away on wings of wax, and the death of Icarus who in his joy flew too close to the sun, have been captured by ancient and modern artists such as Brueghel, Matisse and Picasso.

The contradictory emotions of flying are embodied in these two characters of Greek myth. Daedalus, who managed to imitate the flight of birds and to enjoy the freedom of the sky, is the skillful, cool, meticulous and confident pilot, courageous and in control. He possesses "the right stuff." Icarus, on the other hand, can be seen to represent a nonflyer: unappreciative of the skills required and incapable of handling a life-threatening situation in a steady or detached manner. Lacking his father's caution, Icarus is negligent and, finally, the victim of his own emotions.

Daedalus, viewed by the ancients as a godlike figure, is thus transformed into the modern aviator who traverses the skies at will—and finally into the astronaut who flies to the moon, fulfilling humanity's oldest quest. Icarus is the flawed mortal weighed down by gravity, alien to the idea of freedom in space. He cannot accept the new sensory experiences flying brings, and remains tied to his early forebears.

Passengers, by virtue of their passivity on board, might seem relegated to the role of Icarus. But you can "switch to Daedalus mode" if you are prepared to gain an understanding of the airborne environment. One obvious route to this understanding is to learn more about "the sharp end" of flying, the cockpit.

To be on the flightdeck while taking off, landing or a maneuvering through clouds supplies you with invaluable experience. Another remarkable event is to watch an aircraft execute a U-turn in dense cloud cover in order to emerge in the right direction for the runway. Each member of the flightdeck crew carries out his or her duty in this piece of "instrument flying," calling out information at specified intervals. Finally, on cue, the aircraft emerges into the open at the correct altitude and direction for the landing.

Another pathway to understanding is to practice aviation health—what I've called "flying healthy" in this book. You may not be in control of the aircraft but you can be in control of your own body. Once you understand the unusual demands (both physical and psychological) that flying makes on your body, you can do what it takes to experience a near-perfect flight. I have tried in this book to act as your instructor, to enable you to become an active flyer.

The Icarus Complex

✈

There is a significant fact about Icarus that passengers should know, as each of them will experience it to some degree at some time or other. This is the primitive fear of falling I mentioned earlier—our identification of heights with danger. It is apparent in the way some passengers grip their armrests with such pressure that their knuckles turn white when they leave terra firma on take-off.

In certain people, the fear of flying can reach such an intensity that it can be considered excessive. For them, it could be appropriate to call the fear an "Icarus complex," or phobia.

It is a complicated and unusual phobia, incorporating at least six different fears and striking even when sufferers have seemingly been "cured" of it. The most revealing aspect of the Icarus complex, however, is that it appears to affect such a large percentage of the population. One epidemiological survey of anxiety has found that the prevalence throughout the world of all anxiety disorders is between 2.9 and 8.4 percent. Yet when studies are undertaken on the fear of flying, the percentages reach two digits and can be as high as 44 percent (as one U.S. Gallup Poll reported).

One conclusion that could be drawn from this statistic is that the Icarus complex is not a "true" anxiety disorder (because it affects so many people), but something quite different. Perhaps it originates in people's unwillingness to accept or fully understand the fulfilment of the dream of flight. They are quite content to stay rooted to the earth, and turn their backs on the experience and joy of flying. Essentially, they do not understand or desire to understand the medium of the air. In their indifference to flying they have lost the sense of wonder known to early humanity, dreaming of flight.

We have managed the conquest of the air and space, but to experience the exhilaration and power that this success brings we must make the effort to understand and appreciate it. On a practical level, we could perhaps learn to pilot a plane, to glide or parachute. Books, too, can help open up the skies: *The Spirit of St. Louis* (Charles Lindbergh), *Jonathan Livingston Seagull* (Richard Bach), *Wind, Sand and Stars* (Antoine de

Saint-Exupéry), *Carrying the Fire* (Michael Collins) and *The Right Stuff* (Tom Wolfe) all describe the thrill that flying can and should engender.

Or perhaps we may be fortunate enough to participate in one of the most memorable events in aviation: a trip aboard *Concorde*. On this supersonic aircraft you will see the curvature of the earth at 58,000 feet. With one glance, a person can see a quarter of a million square miles. It is the only chance most of us have to fly in a high-performance jet and break the sound barrier, as military pilots do countless times.

The story of Daedalus and Icarus continues to enthral us, because it encapsulates the twin forces of fear and joy: the joy of escaping from the prison of the earth—representing freedom, exhilaration, and a sense of the divine—pitted against the fear of falling—representing failure, the shock of the new and different, and the fear of setting out across uncharted territory.

The choice is yours. Humanity has used wheels to move over land, hulls to move over water and only this century wings to move through the air. Tap into the energy of successful flight and experience the joy. You will become an active flyer and, above all, arrive in better shape.

Appendix A

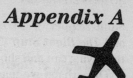

TABLES

Table 1: Alcohol Content of Various Drinks

Alcohol	Type	Units (1 unit = 8 grams of pure alcohol)
Beer (canned)	Export	2.5 units
	Ordinary	1.5–2 units
	Strong	3–4 units
	Extra Strong	4–5 units
Cider (glass)	Ordinary	3 units
	Strong	4–8 units
Cocktails (glass)		1 unit
Wine (glass)		7 units
Spirits (whisky, bourbon, gin, vodka, rum, etc.) (glass)		30 units

Source: MacFarlane, A. and McPherson, A., *The Virgin Now Boarding* . . . (Arrow, 1992)

Table 2: Boeing Cabin Air Flow Data

Flight Deck *entilation Rate/CFM*				*Passenger Cabin Ventilation Rate/CFM*		
Airplane	Fresh	Recirc	Total	Fresh	Recirc	Total
727–100	240	0	240	2200	0	2200
727–200	240	0	240	2600	0	2600
737–200	140	0	140	1500	0	1500
737–300	130	0	130	1300	900	2100
737–400	160	0	160	1500	1800	3300
737–500	130	0.	130	1300	900	2200
747–100	300	140	440	4300	4600	8900
747–200	300	140	440	4300	4600	8900
747–300	290	150	440	4300	5300	9600
747SP	300	140	440	4300	3900	8200
757–200	370	0	370	1500	1700	3200
767–200	250	500	2200	2200	2200	4400

Source: *Boeing*, 1993

Table 3: Ratings of Complaints of Air Quality on Board Aircraft

Cockpit Crew	Cabin Crew	Passenger
1. Humidity	Smoke	Smoke
2. Odor from galley	CO_2*	CO_2*
3. Ozone	Ozone	Humidity
4. –	Humidity	Human Odor
5. –	Bacteria	Ozone
6. –	Human Odor	Bacteria
7. –	Dust[+]	Dust[+]

* CO_2 is reported as "stuffy air" or "lack of oxygen."
[+] Dust comes mainly from the carpets and upholstery.

Source: *Swissair*, 1991

Table 4: Airline Cabin Contaminants

Particulate	Gases
Dust	Organic vapors
Fibers	Odors
ETS (droplets)	ETS (vapors)
Skin flakes	CO_2
Bacteria	O_3
Viruses	(Water)

Source: Pall Corporation, 1991

Table 5: *Aircraft Cabin Air Filtration System: Particle Count Analysis*

Filter efficiency	Particles per cubic meter
50%	47,600
97%	2,200
99.9%	71
99.99%	7
Recirculation ratio is constant at 50%	

Source: Adapted from Pall Corporation, 1991

Table 6: Data on the SST

Concorde is the world's only supersonic passenger aircraft. *British Airways* and *Air France* each have a fleet of the delta-wing jets, with seven and six aircraft respectively. It has crossed the Atlantic in the record time of under three hours (2 hours, 54 minutes and 45 seconds to be precise!).

Capacity: 100 passengers and 1,300 pounds of cargo
Flight Crew: Two pilots and a flight engineer
Cabin Crew: Six
Cruising Speed: 1336 mph (Mach 2) at 55,000 feet
Range: 4,025 miles
Maximum Take-off Weight: 185 tons
Introduction into Service: 1976

Table 7: Typical Menu on the Space Shuttle

Breakfast	Lunch	Dinner
Dried peaches (IM)	Ham (T, I)	Cream of mushroom soup (R)
Sausage (R)	Cheese spread (T)	Smoked turkey (T, I)
Scrambled eggs (R)	Bread (NF, I)	Mixed Italian vegetables (R)
Cornflakes (R)	Green beans and broccoli (R)	Vanilla Pudding (T,R)
Cocoa (B)	Crushed pineapple (T)	Strawberries (R)
Orange-pineapple drink (B)	Shortbread cookies (NF)	Tropical punch (B)
Bananas (FD)	Cashew Nuts (NF)	
	Lemon tea (B)	

Source: Adapted from R. Harding, 1989, by F. Kahn

Legend: B = beverage, I = irradiated, IM = intermediate moist

NF = natural form, FD = freeze-dried, R = rehydratable and T = thermostabilized.

NB:Liquefied condiments (salt, pepper, mustard, ketchup and mayonnaise) are supplied in serving-sized packs.

Table 8: *Contents of U.S. Medical Kits:*
Minimum Requirements

1 × Sphygmomanometer
3 × Oropharyngeal airways
4 × Syringes
6 × Needles
1 × Stethoscope
Epinephrine 1:1000 (2 doses)
10 × Nitroglycerin tablets
2 × Diphenhydramine injectable
50% Dextrose (50 ml)
1 × Instruction Booklet

Source: *Journal of the American Medical Association*
(vol. 262, no. 12, 1989), p. 1654

Table 9: List of Common In-Flight Illnesses

Alcohol abuse
Allergic reactions
Angina
Anxiety reaction
Asthma
Burns
Cholecystitis (inflammation of the gall-bladder)
Dehydration
Diabetes
Enteritis (inflammation of the intestine)
Epistaxis (nose bleeds)
Flu syndrome
Myocardial infarction (heart disease)
Pneumonia
Pulmonary embolism (lung disease)
Renal colic (kidney stone reaction)
Seizures
Syncope (fainting)
Urinary tract infection

Source: *Journal of the American Medical Association* (Cottrell *et al.*; vol 262, no. 12, 1989), p. 1655

Table 10: Composition of the Atmosphere/ Air in the Lungs

Atmosphere	Lungs (Dry Alveolar Air)
Nitrogen (N_2) 78%	Nitrogen (N_2) 80%
Oxygen (O_2) 21%	Oxygen (O_2) 14.5%
Carbon Dioxide (CO_2) 0.03%	Carbon Dioxide (CO_2) 5.5%
Inert Gases (Argon, etc.) 0.97%	

Source: AGARD NATO, 1972

Table 11: U.K. Radiation Doses

Natural	%	Man-made	%
Radon gas from the ground	50	Medical equipment	14
		Radioactive fallout	0.2
Gamma rays from the ground and buildings	14	Miscellaneous, including consumer goods (like luminous dials) and air travel	0.1
Radioactive materials in food and drink	11.5	Work (e.g., non-coal mining, nuclear industry & aircrew)	0.3
Cosmic rays	10	Nuclear discharges from nuclear plants, universities and hospitals	0.1
	85		15

Source: National Radiological Protection Board, 1993

Table 12: *Fuselage Weight and Fuel Penalties Incurred by Pressurizing the Cabins of Aircraft to Sea Level*

Aircraft	Normal Cabin Differential	Sea-level Cabin Differential	Cruise Altitude	Range in Nautical Miles	Fuselage Weight Penalty	Fuel Penalty
Boeing 747–400	8.9 psi	12.6 psi	45,000 feet	3,000 (7,000max)	4,353 lb (6%)	4,000 lb
BAe 146	6.5 psi	10.3 psi	30,000 feet	1,000	563.5 lb (5.8%)	100 lb
Gulfstream IV	9.45 psi	12.6 psi	45,000 feet	3,000	400 lb (5.2%)	60 lb

Source: British Aerospace Airbus, 1994

Table 13: Oxygen Canisters on Board Aircraft
(number of canisters in brackets)

747-400	(30)
767	(16–17)
757	(14)
DC-10	(13)
737	(10)
Airbus 320	(9)
Concorde	(6)

Source: *British Airways,* 1994

Appendix B

SELECTED LIST OF SUPPLIERS

AROMATHERAPY ESSENTIAL OILS
   Danièle Ryman Boutique
   87 Charlwood Street
   London SW1V 4PB
   Tel: 0171–821-7841
   Fax: 0171–931-7334

   Neal's Yard
   1A Rossiter Road
   Balham
   London SW12 9RY
   Tel: 0181–675 7144

HUMIDIFLYER
   Humidiflyer Technologies
   PO Box 168
   Neutral Bay
   NSW 2089
   Australia

PRESSURE OR GAMOW BAG

France:
Certec
Sourcieux-les-Mines 69210
L'Arbresle
France
Tel: 74 70 39 82

U.K.:
Dr. Charles Clarke
UIAA Mountain Centre
St. Bartholomew's Hospital
London EC1A 7BE
Tel: 0171–359 6412

USA:
Portable Hyperbasics
PO Box 510
Ilion, New York 13357
Tel: (315) 895–7485
Price: $1,900, or rent for $250 per month

British Aerospace Airbus
PO Box 55
Filton
Bristol BS99 7AR
Tel: 01272 693 831

Flight Simulators
British Airways
PO Box 10
Heathrow Airport
Hounslow
Middlesex TW6 2JA
Tel: 0181–562 5356

Index

Note: Bold numbers indicate major section

FARROL S. KAHN is the Director of the Aviation Health Institute in the United Kingdom and the author of four books on health and air travel.